# Faith in a Nuclear Age

*A Christian Response to War*

# Faith in a Nuclear Age

*A Christian Peace Shelf Selection*

*Duane Beachey*

*Foreword by Ted W. Engstrom*

HERALD PRESS
Scottdale, Pennsylvania
Kitchener, Ontario
1983

**Library of Congress Cataloging in Publication Data**

Beachey, Duane, 1948-
  Faith in a nuclear age.

  (A Christian peace shelf selection)
  Includes bibliographical references.
  1. Christianity and war.    2. Atomic warfare—Religious
aspects—Christianity.    I. Title.    II. Series: Christian
peace shelf selection.
BT736.2.B4 1983      261.8'73      82-11785
ISBN 0-8361-3308-0 (pbk.)

FAITH IN A NUCLEAR AGE
Copyright © 1983 by Herald Press, Scottdale, Pa.  15683
    Published simultaneously in Canada by Herald Press,
    Kitchener, Ont.  N2G 4M5
Library of Congress Catalog Card Number: 82-11785
International Standard Book Number: 0-8361-3308-0
Printed in the United States of America
Design by David Hiebert
83 84 85 86 87 88 10 9 8 7 6 5 4 3 2 1

To all the world I would say:
God calls you to destroy your machines of war,
    To leave your violent occupations,
    And find your security in him alone.

I don't expect the whole world cares what God wants.
    So to all who *do* care,
        And sincerely seek his better way,
        I dedicate this book.

## Acknowledgments

I especially thank Mary Ann Kennedy and Janet Knisely for their help in typing my manuscript. I also thank Eddy Hall for his invaluable help with my writing. And to the many, many others who read the manuscript and offered hundreds of helpful suggestions and corrections and encouragement—thank-you.

Duane Beachey

# Contents

# *Foreword*

Whenever two or more people discuss "a Christian response to war," there will be differences of opinion. This is a complex and controversial issue. However, it is hard to think of a topic that deserves more careful study by thoughtful Christians these days. I am grateful for the valuable contribution in this arena that Duane Beachey offers to us in *Faith in a Nuclear Age*.

We need to learn all that we can about biblical positions and understandings related to peacemaking in our troubled world. The church must face the issues honestly as it struggles to respond to the awesome realities of the nuclear arms race. As thinking Christians, how are we to relate to nuclear weaponry and all that it represents in the light of biblical teaching on war, peace, and universal human rights? Beachey helps us understand both the biblical mandates and the political realities of our time.

Each of us, as individuals and as part of the corporate body of Christ, needs to determine what it means to be faithful to Christ in the present situation. The author helps us in this struggle. We may not fully agree with his conclusions, but each of us certainly will be challenged to review carefully our own convictions on these matters.

With the advent of nuclear weaponry, the church must provide both faithful political reasoning and moral integrity. Beachey presents options for us to consider—and perhaps debate. He insists that responsible Christians need to sort out their societal priorities and pray that God will be glorified by the peacemaking efforts of his people.

*Faith in a Nuclear Age* thoughtfully considers war and peace in both the Old and New Testaments, pacifism and the arms race, some options available for peacemaking, the theological basis for peacemaking, what is meant by a "just war," the psychology of our nuclear age, and many similar key topics.

Beachey's incisive material provides strong assistance for exploring key social/ethical issues from within the framework of our shared evangelical and biblical faith. His style is readable and enjoyable as well as provocative.

I particularly appreciate the author's honesty and candor in discussing an issue which is ignored by far too many who name the name of Christ. Insisting that each of us must study the Bible honestly, Beachey does this for himself, and shares his insights with us.

I am neither a Mennonite nor a committed pacifist, but I am grateful for the sensitive treatment of a controversial issue within our evangelical community and the useful distinction the author makes between being a pacifist and a "peacemaker." This difference needs to be carefully understood.

It is not necessary to agree fully with an author's conclusions to appreciate what he says and how he says it. I was informed and enlightened by reading this book and I believe a similar experience awaits you. It is needed, timely, and challenging. Each of us will be a better peacemaker as we wrestle with this suggested Christian response to war.

> Ted W. Engstrom, President
> World Vision, Inc.
> Monrovia, California

# Introduction

You will hear of wars and rumors of wars, but
see to it that you are not alarmed. Matthew 24:6.

Wars and rumors of wars fill the news. Many people are gripped by a grim fear—the feeling that not many years are left before the Big One. Hardly anyone expects a peaceful solution to our nuclear arms dilemma. Fear has become a dominant element of our society.

How can Jesus in the midst of all this danger say to us, "See to it that you are not alarmed"? How can we help but be troubled?

Many Christians are becoming concerned—even alarmed—about nuclear weapons. Some who just a few years ago would have supported a strong defense are now calling for disarmament. More and more church leaders are taking a new look at what the Bible says about being peacemakers. Some from churches long silent on the issue of war are speaking out against the arms race—particularly nuclear weapons.

In all this discussion the church needs to hear Jesus' words "See that you are not troubled" and his oft repeated "Fear not."

Christians encounter a dilemma when they call for disarmament precisely because of their fears. They seek in vain for the impossible. They want a middle ground between nuclear arms, which they fear on the one side, and a weak defense against enemies, whom they fear on the other side. Their wish seems to be, "If we could just eliminate nuclear weapons and keep our other defenses, we could feel safe once again." Their wish is impossible because the world can never regain its nuclear innocence. We can't go back. We cannot successfully half defend ourselves or half fight a war.

So how in the world can we keep from being troubled? Let's go back to Jesus and take a look at what else he says. If the old wineskins won't hold the new wine of peacemaking, let's get new wineskins.

Absolute trust in the Father was always central in Jesus' constant admonitions: "Fear not," "Don't be anxious," or "See that you are not troubled." If we can approach Jesus with absolute trust and commit ourselves to follow *wherever* he leads, we will find our fears and anxieties shedding off behind us.

Many Christians have wrestled for years with the issues of war and peacemaking, before they could finally be at peace with their own positions. My own struggle has been to turn Christ's teaching into an alive, personal issue, and more importantly to understand and identify with other Christians who have to struggle with what always seemed self-evident to me in Jesus' teaching.

As a young boy, my deepest feelings about war were captured in two snapshots mixed among the family pictures in our shoebox of photos. They were snapshots of a Japanese family, which my father got from a cousin who fought in the war. He had taken them from a dead soldier's wallet. I looked and looked at that family. They were happy and smiling. It wasn't like war pictures in a magazine. The pictures weren't terrible at all. They were *very* ordinary. It was where they came from that was so terrible!

The pacifism of my Mennonite background, however, was not fed by any easy sentiments of the goodness of all people or "Love conquers all" slogans. Pacifism was no simplistic solution to human conflict. Ours was too long a history of persecution for us to harbor such illusions. Pacifism was by no means the easy road. Jesus said that his was the narrow way and few would find it. We didn't expect therefore that loving one's enemies would be very popular in the world.

It always seemed, however, that within the church, pacifism shouldn't be the minority position. All the basic concepts of what it means to accept and follow Jesus are reflected in many churches and denominations across America. We have the same belief in Jesus' incarnation, ministry, death, and resurrection. Because God came to us in Christ, we all agree that we can repent from our sinful ways, accept God's grace and forgiveness, and walk in a new life by the Holy Spirit's power.

Into this new life we have all been baptized. No longer do we walk in the old ways of greed, anger, and selfishness. Our values are changed. We see the world with new eyes. We pledge to follow Jesus no matter what the cost. So why do we not see our enemy as Jesus sees him? Or rather, why do we differ so radically in how we believe our enemy should be treated? To us Mennonites it seemed clear that if we could only see our enemy, *truly* see him, we could never destroy him.

Many Christians share a belief in the full authority of Scripture. We would never agree to ignore parts of it or explain it away. Yet we cannot agree on how to understand something as simple as Jesus' injunction, "Love your enemies, do good to those who hate you" (Luke 6:27).

Though we don't all agree on how it will happen, we believe that no matter what humans may do, Jesus is going to step decisively into history and establish his reign over all people. Why then do we not agree on the evil of savage struggles to maintain and preserve the kingdoms of this present age—even at times to extend their power? Shouldn't we be building on the kingdom that will not pass away? What are we fearful of losing? The world hasn't given us our peace, our love, our joy; nor can the world take them from us!

We share all these basic concepts of Christ's death for all sinners, the new life of the Christian, the authority of Scripture, Christ's return, our trust in God, and reconciliation, love, peace, long-suffering, forgiveness, meekness, gentleness, and suffering for the sake of righteousness. Because war is so contrary to all these concepts, I have always felt pacifism shouldn't be the minority position in the church.

Of course, recently we have noted a growing interest in pacifism. Because of the nuclear threat church leaders in many denominations are taking a new look at the moral questions involved in war. There is an increased recognition that a nuclear holocaust would be like a hundred Auschwitzes and as such would be the greatest evil beyond the crucifixion that man has ever committed.

But the call to peacemaking is not consistently strong and is often limited to nuclear arms control. I hope this will be a time when Christians look even deeper at the whole issue of war and the military.

When Jesus spoke of being a peacemaker, he was not talking simply of being a pacifist. A pacifist is opposed to war and refuses to participate in it. Jesus meant a great deal more than that. A "peacemaker" actively promotes peace and understanding, and works for what is the basis of any real peace—justice, equality, brotherhood, and at the deepest level, peace with God. What is not so obvious to many Christians is that although "peacemaker" means a great deal more than being a pacifist, it nevertheless includes being a pacifist, or one opposed to war.

Most people in most generations have had to personally face the war issue. This book is not so much a challenge to Christians to stop the nation's war policies, but to stop *participating* in those policies.

I do not intend to set up this issue as a test of who is or is not a Christian; God decides that. I believe, however, that once we clearly see the path to which Christ calls us on this matter, we do not have the option to reject it and still claim to follow him. I intend to carefully state the attitude toward war that I believe most faithfully reflects the way of Jesus Christ, whom all Christians confess as Lord of their lives.

At the deepest level, I believe our attitudes about war will directly affect or reflect our relationships with each other in times of conflict and disagreement. The questions involved in the war issue go to the very heart of our Christian commitment, for they are questions of faith, of obedience, and of love.

Duane Beachey
Spencer, Oklahoma

# Faith
# in a
# Nuclear
# Age

# 1
## Nuclear Arms: A Moral Issue

I know the human race is not going to suddenly be
converted to Christ but that does not keep me from
preaching Him. I also know the nations are not going to
suddenly lay down their arms but that does not keep us
from doing all we can before it is too late.[1]

—Billy Graham

The nation held its breath for thirteen days during
the Cuban missile crisis. Everyone waited anxiously to
see which side would blink first. The Soviets had
repeatedly assured the world that Cuba would not become a missile base. Now the Pentagon had photos of
missile bases under construction in Cuba—the evidence was undeniable.

Robert Kennedy recalled how they explored every
possible avenue of resolving the conflict—how each option was carefully weighed. All the differing opinions
were aired. Military people wanted to bomb the missile
sites immediately. The State Department wanted to ne-
gotiate. Contacts were made with the So-

viets; the Soviets lied about the missiles. Finally, after days of tense meetings, an ultimatum was issued: Agree by tomorrow to remove the missiles, or we will remove them, knowing that you may feel compelled to retaliate.

The Soviets offered to remove them if the United States would remove their missiles from Turkey. The missiles in Turkey were already obsolete and were scheduled to be removed anyway. This would have allowed the Soviets to save some face.

President Kennedy replied: No deal. Remove yours or we will remove them. Then the U.S. officials waited to see what the Soviets would do. They thought they had about a 50—50 chance that the Soviets would back down. And Robert Kennedy tells how his brother talked, during that period of waiting, of the possibility of nuclear war:

> The thought that disturbed him most, and that made the prospect of war much more fearful than it would otherwise have been, was the specter of the death of the children of this country and all the world—the young people who had no role, who had no say, who knew nothing even of the confrontation, but whose lives would be snuffed out like everyone else's. They would never have a chance to make a decision, to vote in an election, to run for office, to lead a revolution, to determine their own destinies.[2]

Khrushchev backed down. The United States agreed not to invade Cuba. The catastrophe was averted. Soon after, Khrushchev was replaced by leaders who were considered to be more hard-nosed.

Some would say "deterrence" worked. Deterrence is the delicate balance by which it is hoped neither side would dare start a war because both sides realize they would be destroyed. The Soviets, under Khrushchev, realized that if a war started, their country would also be destroyed, and so they backed down. In reality, deterrence *didn't* work both ways.

Kennedy, with the full realization of the possible consequences, was not deterred. The fact that the United States wouldn't even "trade" missiles already ordered to be removed suggests a willingness to risk nuclear war in order to retain a macho appearance.

Somehow many of us had imagined that we would only go to war with the Soviets (almost surely involving a nuclear holocaust) if we or our allies were attacked.

## Who Decides Whether a War Is Just?

Many churches have allowed that Christians may fight if the war is just, if the methods are just and not out of proportion to the provocation. But the question can be asked: At what point will Christians no longer support national policy? Any government of this age, not just those under madmen like Hitler, can hardly be trusted to make moral decisions which Christians should automatically obey.

Does anyone today doubt that German Christians in the 1930's were not adequately prepared to deal with the moral issues of Nazi terror? Although the church in general believed and taught that it is right for Christians to fight in wars that are just, it was not teaching Christians to discern what was either a just cause for war or a just means. If the state justified *itself*, the church largely remained silent. To do otherwise was dangerous, as some found out. Thus, Christian German soldiers confronted what would probably be the most important and difficult moral decisions they would ever face. They had little more preparation or guidance than their non-Christian companions.

Many churches today still give their young people little ethical guidance on the issue of war. They teach mostly patriotism, nationalism, and total obedience.

## An Urgent Moral Issue

If the government required all medical doctors to perform abortions on demand, there is little doubt that hundreds or even thousands of Christian doctors would refuse. Some would break the law; others would leave the medical profession. The reason is that the church has been thinking seriously about abortion. Much of the church has now reached somewhat of a consensus that abortion is immoral and that it is an urgent ethical issue of our time.

The issue of nuclear weapons is in many respects far more urgent and certainly more far-reaching than the issue of abortion. While abortion destroys millions of innocent lives, nuclear weapons may well destroy hundreds of millions. Our efforts to end abortion will largely affect only our own nation; our efforts to reduce the nuclear threat affect the whole world. Abortion threatens the lives of many people individually; nuclear arms threaten the very existence of civilization.

The hour is already late. The church desperately needs to seriously study, pray, and teach about this moral issue. The church cannot simply continue to hope that deterrence will work indefinitely, that neither side will dare to fire. Billy Graham in an interview said:

> I know that some people feel human beings are so terrified of a nuclear war that no one would dare start one. I wish I could accept that. But neither history nor the Bible gives us much reason for optimism. What guarantee is there that the world will never produce another maniacal dictator like Hitler or Amin?

> As a Christian I take sin seriously, and the Christian should be the first to know that the human heart is deceitful and desperately wicked, as Jeremiah says. We can be capable of unspeakable horror, no matter how educated or technically sophisticated we are. Auschwitz is a compelling witness to this.[3]

Once the church has faced the issue, not everyone will come to the same conclusions I have. Nor will we all agree on what our response should be. But these disagreements should not blind us to the central moral issue of an arms race that threatens human civilization and existence. Again the abortion discussion helps clarify the issue.

## No Easy Solutions

Although a consensus seems to have emerged on the immorality of abortion, there is much less consensus on what response is appropriate for *dealing* with the immorality of abortion. Some are actively involved in political action to influence legislation; others don't feel Christians should impose their morals on everyone. Some want to see abortion dealt with as murder; others feel this response is too vindictive and focuses too much on punishment. Some point out the hypocrisy in a large organized Christian movement to end abortion, without a simultaneous movement to adopt or care for the millions of unwanted babies that will result. (Some of the most vocal Christians opposing abortion are also demanding cuts in welfare and food programs for children of the poor.)

But in spite of the differences in our response, the gray areas, a certain degree of hypocrisy and inconsistencies, we largely agree on the basic moral issue involved in abortion. Unborn human life is sacred, and to destroy it is immoral.

In the same way, as we study the moral implications of the nuclear arms race, we will have disagreements in what our response should be. There will be certain gray areas. There will be some hypocrisy. We can easily see the evil of nuclear arms because they threaten *us*, and only dimly see the deeper issues of economic oppression and greed. This greed undergirds our affluent way of life and leads to instability, revolution, terrorism, and war.

We hope for solutions that won't be costly for ourselves, but the problem before us will have no cheap solutions. Whether we ignore it or face it, whether we go for easy solutions or make the tough decisions, I believe the issue of nuclear arms and how we deal with our enemies will be difficult. Christians should once again look seriously at what Jesus meant about loving enemies, trusting the Father, and taking up a cross.

### Studying the Bible Honestly

We must study the Scriptures with great seriousness, not just grabbing for verses here and there to prove a point. I believe the best way to guard against that tendency in all of us is to pray for discernment. We must sincerely ask one question: "If Jesus were sitting here teaching me, what would he most likely say about this Scripture?" Even then our scriptural interpretations will not always agree, but we might guard against straying so far apart at times.

For example, I was listening to a well-known television preacher, who was preaching from Isaiah. He was emphasizing Isaiah's call for the nation to repent and come back to God. The two major areas where he felt we had gone wrong as a nation were our ever increasing welfare system and the way we had allowed our military defenses to slip behind those of Russia.

If he had studied the book of Isaiah a little more deeply and applied its message with more consistency, he would have seen that the prophet also speaks to these issues. The first issue Isaiah hammers at again and again: You have failed to properly care for the poor in your midst. "... wash and make yourselves clean. Take your evil doings out of my sight! Stop doing wrong, learn to do right! Seek justice, encourage the oppressed. Defend the cause of the fatherless, plead the case of the widow." In the next verse Isaiah adds the call to repentance which we hear so often, but too seldom connect to these issues of justice and mercy for orphans and widows, ".Come now, let us reason together,' says the Lord. 'Though your sins are like scarlet, they shall be as white as snow; though they are as red as crimson, they shall be like wool' " (Isaiah 1:16-18).

Regarding military preparedness, Isaiah also calls Israel to repent. He berates them for putting their trust in the strength and numbers of their arms and the power of their allies: "Woe to those who go down to Egypt for help, who rely on horses, who trust in the multitude of their chariots and in the great strength of their horsemen, but do not look to the Holy One of Israel, or seek help from the Lord" (Isaiah 31:1).

The television preacher had not just slightly changed the emphasis. He had taken Isaiah's message of repentance and turned it completely upside down! This is what I mean by studying the Scripture seriously. If the preacher had asked what Jesus would most likely say, could he possibly imagine Jesus rebuking us for spending too much on welfare for dependent children and the disabled, and too little for military weapons?

## In the World, but Not of the World

Whenever Christians find themselves echoing secular concerns, they need to look very carefully at the issues. We won't always be at odds with secular concerns, but we should keep our eyes open. Christians have generally believed that they are called to live by a different standard than that of the secular (at times pagan) society around them. The secular world nearly always looks first to its own interests. We expect it to look to the interests of others only if it has something to gain. This approach is exactly opposite from the way that leads to peace.

Later chapters will look more specifically at the biblical teachings concerning the way of peace and the biblical teaching concerning the place of government and our involvement or responsibilities to it. First we might notice some of the more obvious inconsistencies evident in the church today.

### Trusting His Word

Jesus said, "Love your enemies, do good to those who hate you" (Luke 6:27). His phrasing couldn't have been simpler or more straightforward. He offered no exceptions. He throws in no ambiguous phrases like: "as much as you are able." The teaching seems plain. Nonetheless, through most of the history of the church, Christ's followers have been using all kinds of reasoning to show why it doesn't apply to war.

Many churches insist on the authority of the Bible as the guide for our lives. Conservative evangelicals especially have called for interpreting the Scripture as literally as possible. "Liberals" are often accused of interpreting Scripture loosely. One might expect them to reinterpret Jesus' teaching that we should love our enemies to fit the cultural realities of the modern world. Instead, it is most often the conservative evangelicals who explain that either Jesus' teachings aren't realistic in a fallen and evil world or they don't apply beyond personal relationships.

### Trusting the Father

Jesus said a great deal about trusting the Father. The Old Testament prophets also had words of judgment against trusting in the strength of arms and alliances.

Yet many Christians insist that our military strength be superior to every other nation's. Continually we trust our arms to maintain a secure place for us in the world.

## Trusting His Return

Perhaps the greatest paradox among evangelical Christians is their insistence that Christ's return and the rapture of the church is *very* near indeed, that this age is rapidly passing. And still they view our dwindling prestige and power in the world with great concern and alarm. At times they actually equate our lack of military resolve and forcefulness with a loss of Christian conviction. Our unwillingness to arm ourselves "to the teeth" is seen as a sign of *un*faithfulness! Can we possibly think that God's purposes in the world hinge on the strength of our arms? Do we imagine that the Omnipotent King of Heaven, who delights in exalting the weak and bringing low the mighty, is grieved if our military strength is not number one in the world?

## Internal Contradictions

These inconsistencies are not the same as those due to the common weakness of all flesh. These are not the same inconsistencies as saying, "I know I should spend more time with my family, but I just don't" or "I know I shouldn't smoke, but I do." In those cases our teaching and our convictions are clear and unambiguous. We just fail to live up to our ideals.

The inconsistencies of the churches' attitude to war are internal contradictions. What most of the church has taught about war is little different from the teaching of secular society. The church's position on war seems to be in contradiction with what this same church has taught about Jesus' teachings, trust in God, interpretation of Scripture, and the return of Christ.

# 2
## *The "Just War"*

For a better understanding of how the church at large formed its attitudes toward arms and violence, let's look briefly at a short history of the church's struggle with the issue. The early church was unified in its teaching against believers participating in warfare. There was apparently less unity in their *practice*. The few soldiers in the early church were evidently already soldiers when they became Christians. New converts were forbidden to enter the forces. Some soldiers faced martyrdom in their attempt to leave the army. At any rate, "no Christian writer before Constantine's reign justified the participation of believers in warfare. Every writer who commented on this—and lots of them did—condemned it."[1]

Scripture, and not the early church's tradition, is our guide for belief and practice. Yet the early church is our common Christian heritage. The early Christians lived near the time of Christ and the apostles, and some had heard the apostles teach. They may more accurately portray the apostles' intentions. We should at least consider what they taught as seriously as we do the teachings of Augustine several centuries later.

The early church was an alive and growing community of believers. In the church they sought to demonstrate a new social order that was faithful to the teachings of Christ. This new order reached across ethnic, cultural, and class barriers. This community was not attempting to gain control over Rome or make the government more moral. Although they lived in the world, their allegiance was to a higher kingdom.

Paul says: "For though we live in the world, we do not wage war as the world does. The weapons we fight with are not the weapons of the world" (2 Corinthians 10:3-4). Elsewhere he says: "If it is possible, as far as it depends on you, live at peace with everyone.... 'If your enemy is hungry, feed him; if he is thirsty, give him something to drink'.... Do not be overcome by evil, but overcome evil with good" (Romans 12:18-21).

Other early Christian leaders, as noted by J. C. Wenger in his booklet *The Way of Peace*, made similar statements. Ignatius (AD 50-115), bishop of Antioch and a martyr, taught that Christians should not seek revenge on those who injure them. Justin the Martyr (AD 100-165) taught that Christians once filled with war will convert their weapons—swords into plowshares and spears into farming implements.

Tertullian (AD 160-225), a lawyer and a Christian, thought Christians should not take part in warfare since the Lord proclaimed that he who uses the sword shall perish by the sword. Tertullian insisted that if a soldier becomes a Christian believer, he must leave the army at once. Origen (AD 185-254), a writer and teacher from Alexandria, Egypt, wrote:

We have come in accordance with the counsels of Jesus to cut down our warlike and arrogant swords of argument into ploughshares, and we convert into sickles the spears we formerly used in fighting. For we no longer take sword against nation, nor do we learn any more to make war, having become sons of peace for the sake of Jesus.[2]

These statements express the general teaching of the church to the time of the emperor Constantine (AD 306-337), a mighty military man, who bestowed many favors on the church. He did not become a Christian himself until on his deathbed, but he convened and chaired the great church Council of Nicaea. He made observance of the Lord's day an imperial regulation and gave large sums for the building of churches.

## An About-Face

Under Constantine, Christian leaders for the first time saw the possibility of making a secure place for the church in the world. Suddenly, from an oft persecuted minority position, the church had gained the position of insiders. When that happened, the church reversed its stand on military service and warfare. All of the important church leaders were quick to declare that Christians might now take life in wartime.

Athanasius (AD 296-372)—bishop of Alexandria, renowned defender of orthodoxy—was often bold in taking unpopular stands for the truth as he saw it. He was opposed to personal killing, but felt that "to kill one's adversary in war is both lawful and praiseworthy." Ambrose (AD 340-397), bishop of Milan, praised soldiers who fought for their homeland. Such courage, he said, is "full of righteousness."

Augustine (AD 354-430), bishop of Hippo in North Africa, is known as the most influential of all leaders of the ancient church.

To his great dismay he saw Rome captured and looted by the Germanic Visigoths in 410. He was deeply shaken, and profoundly concerned that civilization should not collapse. (However, the Western Roman Empire fell in 476, in spite of efforts to save it.) Perhaps this contributed to the vigor with which he declared that it was right for Christians to serve in the military. It was Bishop Augustine who proposed and developed the concept that some wars are "just." This concept has soothed the consciences of Christians on both sides of every war since his time![3]

## The "Just War"

Because Augustine has been so important in forming the church's attitude toward war even today, several points need to be made concerning the "just war." The idea of a just war is based more on secular philosophy than on biblical teaching. In history virtually every country that has gone to war has considered its cause just. How can a party in a dispute judge its own case objectively? Furthermore, if the church will support "just" wars, the implication is that the church would also consider some wars to be *unjust* and would call on Christians not to support those wars. Again, history shows us that this hasn't happened.

As the just war theory has developed, not only is the *cause* for war to be just; but also war is to be the last resort. It is to be against military targets and not innocent women and children. It is not to inflict greater damage on the enemy than their injustice warranted. At an earlier time, when great armies met on the battlefield to do battle, these concepts may have applied. In the nuclear age they hardly apply at all. Our defense strategy depends on nuclear warheads aimed at Russian cities.

Our nation fully intends—has plans—to destroy *millions* of innocent people if sufficiently threatened or aggravated. Some may feel justified in saying that Russia would do the same to us; but if a murderer killed my mother, no one would feel I was justified in killing his mother.

Augustine certainly did not settle the question of war for all time. With the Reformation came a new emphasis on the Scriptures and a reevaluation of traditions. The Reformers also struggled anew with the problems of war and violence.

## The Reformers

In 1520, when Luther was trying to bring renewal to the Catholic Church, he made the following reply to John Eck, a physician:

> You say that I would give room to the peacebreakers and murderers because I have taught that a Christian should abstain from violence and should not fight to recover his belongings of which he has been robbed. Why do you not rebuke Christ who has taught this?[4]

But when the local peasant revolt came, he set aside these convictions and urged the German princes to crush them ruthlessly.

Zwingli, the great Swiss Reformer, had served as a military chaplain and he hated war. In 1522 he said: "Considered from a Christian point of view it is by no means right to have a part in war. According to Christ's teaching we should pray for those who despitefully use us and persecute us." He too joined the military forces and was even killed in battle.

John Calvin, the Reformed leader of Geneva, made the following statement about the passage in Matthew 5:44-45, which speaks of loving our enemies so that we may be the children of our Father in heaven:

> When He expressly declares that no man will be a child of God unless he *loves those who hate him*, who shall dare to say that we are not bound to observe this doctrine? The statement amounts to this, "Whoever shall wish to be ac-

counted a Christian, let him *love his enemies.*" It is truly horrible and monstrous that the world should have been covered with such a thick darkness for three or four centuries as not to see that it is an express command, and that everyone who neglects it is struck out of the number of the children of God.[5]

Yet Calvin, too, when he became part of the religious government of Geneva, decided it was his duty to forcefully drive out heretics.

It seems that many church leaders who have taken a hard look at Jesus' life and teachings have concluded that Christians should renounce war and the preparation for war. But, generally, when the real test came, they felt safer with a sword than with the Father's way of loving enemies. If they were outnumbered and overpowered, they would die boldly; but when it looked as if fighting would give them a chance, they took the sword. Jesus simply submitted to the evil forces, even though he could have called on a whole army of angels. His resurrection is the proof that his was the way of the Father. "Love your enemies ... that you may be the children of your Father in heaven."

## Seeing Through the Old Lies

After so many centuries we should be able to see through the lies concerning warfare, and to see the satanic nature of those lies. The lie that we can protect Christ's gospel of a new order with the methods of the old order. The lie of the "just war," when we see that virtually every war of every nation has been portrayed as a just war. The lie that war can establish peace. The lie that war is a political issue outside the personal spiritual concerns of Christians.

Somehow many Christians have felt they are not personally responsible for what they do in the "service" of the nation. Although war may be considered a sin, being a soldier is not. In no other area do we make such a distinction. If adultery is sin, engaging in adultery is sinful. If greed is a sin, ignoring the needs of the poor while we have plenty is sinful.

## Politics and Religion

There will be those who feel that war is not an issue on which Christians should get "hung up"; they feel that it is a political question or a question of individual conscience. If so, we need only remember again the holocaust of World War II. After the war many asked: Where was the voice of the church in Germany? Where were the German Christians?

When the smoke, rubble, and fallout settle after the threatened nuclear holocaust, if anyone survives, we can be sure they will be asking: Where was the church while this most monstrous sin of all time was being built bomb by bomb? A concerned Christian church cannot honestly hide from this issue because we don't want to think about it, or because it's too controversial, or too complicated. If war is a moral issue, then it is God's concern and must also be the concern of God's people.

## Why Must We Fight?

The following chapters will look at some of the most common reasons why Christians have fought their nation's enemies when they have felt threatened or endangered. Christians use the Old Testament to show that God has sometimes commanded his people to fight. They may agree wholeheartedly that war is evil, but argue that it is the lesser of two evils. They may show how the enemy is bent on domination, opposed to freedom, and antichurch. The hard "reality" of an evil world tells Christians that if we aren't strong and prepared to fight, our way of life will be destroyed. Common sense says that Christians should therefore fight and defeat the nation's enemies.

Other Christians may remind us that the apostle Paul says we are to be obedient to the government and that the government is ordained of God to punish the wicked. When the government calls us to serve in the military, then, they say, we must serve. Others may feel we have too long a tradition of supporting war, and we can't expect the church to change much. Finally, there may be those who personally agree with a pacifist position, but feel that emphasizing it would be too divisive and would hinder spreading the basic gospel message. We will examine these arguments more closely.

# 3
# *War*
# *in the Old Testament*

During wars seen as true threats to national existence, churches have supported participation by drawing analogies to Israel's wars in the Old Testament. The comparison may simply be between the "rightness" of our side and the "rightness" of Israel's defense against foreign and heathen threats. Or the analogies may actually be used to declare a particular war a "holy war" and to call Christians to join in God's battle against the evil forces of the world. World War I is an example of a war which many churches raised to the level of "holy war." It was proclaimed "the war to end all wars!" We see now how futile it was to hope that a war could end war.

## The Old Testament as a Guide

The Old Testament wars are interpreted and understood in many ways. Entire books have been written on the subject. Before we look at the Old Testament, we should first note that in no other major areas of social or religious behavior do Christians generally use the Old Testament in favor of the New. The Old Testament is not our guide for marriage. Polygamy is considered heathen. In civil law, capital punishment for adultery is considered excessively harsh. We no longer follow the ceremonial laws or worship patterns. Even in matters of war we have never heeded the consistent Old Testament warning against military alliances with foreign governments.

## Israel, a Theocracy

There are other differences between our nation and its wars, and ancient Israel and her wars. Some have tried to portray our nation as God's new "chosen people." Such a comparison to Israel seems forced, especially to Christians in other nations. Israel was a theocracy, a nation ruled by God. The prophets played a major role in the policies and decisions of Israel. Although some would call ours a Christian nation, and our pledge says "under God," we could hardly be considered a theocracy.

## Fighting from Weakness

We do not fight wars in the same way Israel fought. In addition to speaking against alliances, the prophets also spoke against placing trust in the strength and numbers of military power. The most memorable battles under Joshua and Gideon were fought from weakness rather than strength. Israel simply marched, sang, or blew trumpets; and God caused the walls to fall, threw the enemy into confusion, or sent a hailstorm.

We, on the other hand, have always trusted our power or our cunning strategy. And many Christians today feel strongly that our military forces should be second to none. Some actually imply that any signs of weakness in our military demonstrate a loss of faithfulness to God. This is exactly opposite to the position of the Old Testament prophets. To the prophets many of Israel's wars were not holy wars at all. They were acts of disobedience—not allowing God to fight the battle, but doing it their way. Isaiah 31:1-3 says:

> Woe to those who go down to Egypt for help, who rely on horses, who trust in the multitude of their chariots and in the great strength of their horsemen, but do not look to the Holy One of Israel, or seek help from the Lord.... But the Egyptians are men and not God; their horses are flesh and not spirit. When the Lord stretches out his hand, he who helps will stumble, he who is helped will fall; both will perish together.

Vernard Eller has written an excellent book entitled *War and Peace from Genesis to Revelation.* It deals in depth with the issue of holy war. He says of the above Isaiah passage: "Here Isaiah explicitly brands Israel's military preparedness—her arms and alliances and whatever—as being part of her *sin,* as a particular sign of her failure to trust Yahweh and his promise for Zion and mankind. And this preparedness, it should be pointed out, was totally defensive in character."[1]

In terms of placing trust in powerful arms and alliances, America's wars (or even modern Israel's wars) seem more parallel to Isaiah's situation than to the "holy wars" of Joshua and Gideon, in which God fought the battle.

## Why the Difference
## Between Old and New Testament?

One doesn't need either a scholarly mind or an in-depth study to notice some remarkable differences between the portrayal of God in the Old Testament and his portrayal in the New. This is particularly evident with regard to how enemies are treated. A number of ways have been suggested for explaining these differences.

I will offer only one explanation or suggestion. Undoubtedly, not everyone will be able to accept this approach to the Old Testament. I feel, however, that it has the distinct advantage for Christian believers of taking seriously what Christ taught. It takes seriously the way Jesus interpreted the Old Testament. From that perspective we seek to understand the Old Testament on the question of war. This approach seems better than to stand on an Old Testament teaching and from there try to interpret what Jesus meant.

## The Old Covenant Superceded

In the Old Testament, God's work for man's redemption is seen coming through Israel, a nation-state—God's chosen people. In the New Testament we see God working for man's redemption through Jesus Christ. This is the ultimate reason for not using the Old Testament to justify our wars today. Had the old covenant been God's perfect pattern and plan for our lives, there would have been no reason for a new covenant. Christ would not have needed to come. "For what the law was powerless to do in that it was weakened by the sinful nature, God did by sending his own Son in the likeness of sinful man" (Romans 8:3). Christ *did* come, not to destroy the Law but, as he said, "to fulfill it." In fulfilling the Law he raises us above it. Jesus repeatedly said, "You have heard [from the Law] . . . but I say. . . ."

Through Jesus we can best come to understand the Old Testament. Jesus gives us an important key for understanding and interpreting what seems like a lower standard in the Old Testament. The Pharisees questioned him about divorce: "Why did Moses command that a man give his wife a certificate of divorce and send her away?" Jesus replied, "Moses *permitted* [emphasis added] you to divorce your wives because your hearts were hard. But it was not this way from the beginning" (Matthew 19:3-9). Jesus appealed *past* the Law to God's earlier intent at creation.

## God's Original Intention

Again and again Jesus appealed past the Law to God's intentions in the first place. Not only is murder wrong, as the Law teaches, but so is unrestrained anger. Not only is adultery wrong, but so is the lustful looking at a woman. Not only is it wrong to break an oath, but it is wrong to lie at all. Not only is it wrong to retaliate in any degree beyond the offense or injury received, but we are not even to resist the evil person who injures, bullies, or takes advantage of us. Even more incredibly, we are to love and pray for them (Matthew 5:21-44).

This same principle of God permitting and even ordering things which were not his original intentions are illustrated at several places in the Old Testament. When Israel asked for a king, God told Samuel, "It isn't you they are rejecting but me." Then God proceeded to tell Samuel how to choose the king. God even chose who their king would be, but he did so because of the hardness of their hearts.

Another example of God allowing (or even commanding) what was less than his original intention, may be the sending of the twelve spies into Canaan. The account in Numbers 13 says that God *told* Moses to choose twelve men to spy out the land. But in Deuteronomy 1:21-23 we read that God told them to go into the land and take possession of it. They were not to be afraid. But the people all said, "Let us send men ahead to spy out the land for us." Since "the idea seemed good" to Moses, he chose twelve men and sent them as spies. If the Israelites' doubts and fears caused them to suggest spies, their doubts and fears were only increased by the report of the spies; and they were turned back to the wilderness for forty more years because they doubted.[2]

## Did God Have a Better Plan for Israel?

In Exodus 23:20-23 we find what may have been God's original plan for conquering Canaan. This message from God came shortly after the giving of the Ten Commandments.

> See, I am sending an angel ahead of you to guard you along the way and to bring you to the place I have prepared.... If you listen carefully to what he says and do all that I say, I will be an enemy to your enemies and will oppose those who oppose you.... I will send my terror ahead of you and throw into confusion every nation you encounter. I will make all your enemies turn their backs and run. I will send the hornet ahead of you to drive the Hivites, Canaanites and Hittites out of your way. But I will not drive them out in a single year, because the land would become desolate and the wild animals too numerous for you. Little by little I will drive them out before you, until you have increased enough to take possession of the land.... I will hand over to you the people who live in the land and you will drive them out before you. Do not make a covenant with them or with their gods. Do not let them live in your land, or they will cause you to sin against me.

This sounds as though God planned to do the fighting and Israel was just to move in and push out every vestige of pagan culture as God made room for them little by little. When they first marched into Canaan, God miraculously destroyed the mighty walls of Jericho. The Israelites violently destroyed every living thing in the city. Unlike in later battles, we aren't told that God commanded this action. Very shortly thereafter, disobedience was found among them. And soon after that, without consulting God, the Israelites made a covenant with one of the pagan tribes to let them remain in the land.

We find that after the battle of Jericho God often told Israel to kill every living thing when they conquered a city. Might this command not, again, have been given because of their hardness of heart? At any rate, there is no doubt that God's arm was never too short. From time to time the Israelites were still able to trust him to fight for them as with Gideon. One time they marched into battle doing nothing, but singing praise to God (2 Chronicles 20:21-25). On other occasions God sent a hail of stones (Joshua 10:11) or hornets (Joshua 24:12), and the enemy fled in confusion and fear.

### God Works with Imperfect Israel

As God worked through Israel's kings to build a nation for his chosen people, so he worked through their wars for his purposes once they had decided to fight their own battles. When they completely turned from God to idolatry or to oppression and greed, God used defeats to chasten them and bring them back to following him.

Peter Craigie, in his book *The Problem of War in the Old Testament*, says that "a superficial reading of the Old Testament may result in positive attitudes toward war." A fuller reading, however, shows that: (1) Because of man's nature, violence only leads to violence even with the best of intentions. (2) The truest image of God's purpose in the world, or the truth about God, emerges from Israel's understanding of her defeats, more than from her victories. The suffering Israel more than the conquering Israel became the prophetic image of the suffering servant pointing us to Christ. (3) Throughout the Old Testament the prophecies all pointed to the final vision of peace.[3]

Craigie says that war is always evil and the Old Testament makes no attempt to portray war in a more positive light. All the details of the inherent ruthlessness and cruelty and injustice of war are left in. But God is seen working through imperfect human beings to carry forward his plans for man's final redemption.

David was called "a man after God's own heart," yet he was a great warrior as well as a polygamist. We can no more use David's example as evidence of God's blessing on war than on polygamy! Neither war nor polygamy was God's intention from the beginning.

## The Old Testament Vision of Restored Peace

From creation God's intention has always been for people to be in fellowship with him and at peace with one another. All of God's efforts throughout history have been toward the one purpose of restoring that peace—the peace of the garden, the peace of the New Jerusalem. Humans have used every conceivable method to be at peace with God, but throughout the Bible in many different ways God says: "You can't have peace with me while you treat your brothers and sisters with greed and violence."

The story of Cain and Abel illustrates how seriously God views the taking of human life and being irresponsible for a brother. As people grew increasingly wicked, God despaired of bringing any change except by starting over with the good family of Noah. God said to Noah, "I am going to put an end to all people, for the earth is filled with violence because of them. I am surely going to destroy both them and the earth" (Genesis 6:13). God condemned Noah's contemporaries because of their violence.

Then Noah's descendants drifted from God's way too.

From among them God chose Abram and told him, "All peoples on earth will be blessed through you and your offspring." Years later, from amidst the slavery and despair of Abraham's descendants, God called Moses to lead his people out of Egypt. And God gave them a law to remind them of his purposes. They had a written record of God's plan for a people at peace with one another—a people with concern for the poor and the widows. They were to be a light to the nations—a people with God as king.

God's people took all of God's special favor and claimed it for their own. They forgot that *all* the families of the earth were to be blessed through them. The framework for peace and justice was there. A few, like Isaiah, were able to see the vision—to see the broader scope of God's whole purpose. But the Israelites as a whole, because of their selfish, violent nature, were seldom able to pursue God's purpose of restoring peace in their own land. Even less were they able to work toward restoring peace to the whole world.

# 4
## Jesus' Teaching on Peace

The theme of God's desire for peace can be seen running throughout the Old Testament from creation to the prophets. But through Jesus we see how important peacemaking really is to God. Jesus said, "Blessed are the peacemakers, for they will be called children of God" and "Love your enemies ... that you may be the children of your Father in heaven." Thus, Jesus tied peacemaking and love for our enemies directly into what it means to be a born-again child of God.

We have understood Jesus' saying "You have heard ... but I say ..." as freeing us from the legalism of the Law. We have gladly accepted the freedom from legalism, but the call to a higher way is often accepted only if it seems practical. And "practical" is usually defined as not being too costly, dangerous, foolish, or inconvenient.

## A Future Ethic Only?

Some Christians have put off Jesus' ethical teachings, such as the Sermon on the Mount, as applying to a coming age. But if Jesus' higher ethic is for a future time, then we would remain under the Law which Jesus supercedes. The Sermon on the Mount can hardly be only the ethic of the millennium. In the coming age of peace what sense would it make to say, "Blessed are those who are persecuted because of righteousness, for theirs is the kingdom of heaven. Blessed are you when people insult you, persecute you and falsely say all kinds of evil against you because of me" (Matthew 5:10-11)?

Paul repeats the theme of loving our enemies in Romans 12:20, "If your enemy is hungry, feed him; if he is thirsty, give him something to drink."

Jesus hardly leaves us room to believe that the "eye for an eye, tooth for a tooth" rule still applies in this age for his followers. He placed his Sermon on the Mount squarely into the sociopolitical situation of his own day by telling his followers to carry a soldier's bags two miles if conscripted to carry it one. He said that those who take the sword will perish by the sword. His response to hated occupation soldiers was to heal the servant of a Roman centurion. He ate and visited with tax collectors, who were considered collaborators and traitors. He had Zealots as disciples, but never espoused their beliefs or methods. (The Zealots were a party of deeply religious freedom fighters. They constantly looked for ways to stir up revolution against Rome. They saw the pagan Roman rule as a desecration of their holy land.)

## Christian Zealots

The Zealots might well be compared to the "God and country" Christians of today. If America were under foreign military rule, as Israel was under the rule of Rome, one would expect these Christian patriots to help form an underground resistance. They would even consider such activity as their Christian duty. They would likely be involved in sabotage, guerrilla bands, underground newspapers, and secret meetings to encourage insurrection. This was exactly the Zealot position. Jesus' consistent rejection of their methods is a good indication of his position on the use of violence or force to attain political freedom.

## Really Loving Real Enemies

Immediately following Jesus' admonition to carry a soldier's bags two miles instead of the required one, comes his well-known saying, "Love your enemies and pray for those who persecute you" (Matthew 5:44). His audience could have no illusions that Jesus was only referring to personal relationships. Physical assault, lawsuits, and conscription to serve occupation soldiers are very provoking situations and are charged with political overtones.

Jesus didn't tell his followers to act thus toward their enemies out of expediency because they were outmatched and overpowered. Rather, Jesus went on to say, "that you may be [the children] of your Father in heaven. He causes his sun to rise on the evil and the good, and sends rain on the righteous and the unrighteous.... Be perfect, therefore, as your heavenly Father is perfect" (Matthew 5:45, 48).

## Clearing Temples

If we present Jesus as the peacemaker too diligently, someone will always say: But what about his clearing of the temple? This incident, above all others, is used to show that sometimes Jesus approved of using force (or even violence, depending on how much he actually used his whip) to oppose evil. From this incident we are to conclude that sometimes violence, and even war if necessary, may be used to oppose evil. But would those who use this example feel comfortable even with violent "temple clearing"?

Imagine a bazaar in the basement of a million-dollar church, where well-dressed, wealthy people are boisterously bidding a few dollars in hopes of raising $300 to send to starving people in India; suppose some "prophet" came crashing in, upsetting tables, and shouting about giving *real* offerings. Who would call his actions "Christlike"? Most would say things like: "Who is he to judge?" or "Even if he had a point, that was certainly not the way to make it—he even *hit* some people with a piece of rope!" or "Well, Jesus may have done it, but that man certainly wasn't Jesus, so he shouldn't try to act like it!"

Imagine *any* violent temple-clearing scene today, and ask how many Christians would approve. If we wouldn't feel comfortable using Jesus' method to shake up commercialized, uncompassionate, wealthy churches today, then we shouldn't try to stretch Jesus' "temple clearing" to cover our brutal, deadly, and devastating wars.

This imagined example doesn't fully answer the question of when the use of force such as Jesus used would be applicable. But we might note that his strongest words, as well as his strongest actions, were directed against the injustices of the religious leaders. To those usually considered "the enemy," such as tax collectors and occupation soldiers, he showed only love.

## Not Peace but a Sword

Some claim that Jesus actually supports the use of the sword. For example, Jesus said, "I did not come to bring peace, but a sword" (Matthew 10:34). The context makes clear that here Jesus is simply saying that his followers will suffer persecution. The gospel will meet resistance in the world. It will bring conflict. Of course the experience of the apostles and other believers from then until now has repeatedly fulfilled Jesus' prediction.

Another time Jesus told his disciples, "If you don't have a sword, sell your cloak and buy one" (Luke 22:36). When they responded, "Here are two swords," he replied, "That is enough." I have yet to hear a good explanation of this obscure passage. Later that evening it must have been one of those swords that showed up in Peter's hand—and removed a man's ear. Since Jesus rebuked Peter, he evidently didn't want the sword to be used.

We know that Jesus faced temptations just as we do. On that night he faced what may have been his most serious struggle ever—Gethsemane. Perhaps he struggled with the thought of taking things in his own hands. So he told his disciples, "We'd better be prepared and have some swords, just in case." But when his gung-ho disciples promptly came up with two swords, he must have shaken his head in disbelief at their inability to understand the true nature of the struggle he faced. So with some sarcasm, he said, "That ought to be enough!"

This story throws a curve-ball that would be difficult to convert into an argument either for *or* against the sword. But the overwhelming weight of Jesus' example and teachings demonstrates in the strongest possible terms that he actually expected his disciples to follow him in the way of suffering love. He actually meant for everything he taught to be accepted as the guide for how we are to live. "If anyone loves me, he will obey my teaching" (John 14:23).

Vernard Eller says it so well: Jesus wasn't a philosopher dropping teachings for people to decide which are good ones. Rather, he is *king,* saying, "Follow me."

> And when the King is this one, that obviously will have to entail a career of humble service to one's fellowmen; a readiness in every situation to accept suffering rather than inflict it on another; the willingness to risk defeat and even death in the faith that, if needs be, God can pull off a resurrection to put things right.[1]

## Getting Around the Hard Part

Of course, Bible-believing Christians would usually not decide that certain of Jesus' teachings are good ones and others aren't. They would say that all of his teachings are true! So rather than reject certain teachings, they will simply reduce Jesus' message in various ways.

In general, the teaching to love our enemies has been taken to mean that if our enemies hate us only "in their hearts," then we are to love them in return even in concrete and physical ways. But if they hate us in concrete and physical ways, then we can only love them in return "in our hearts."

Jesus' teaching to love our enemies is often reduced to the personal level, as if that were its only meaning. Thus, we are to treat kindly our grumpy next-door neighbors. But on the international level we are told that we are not personally responsible to treat enemies the Jesus way and we may even personally involve ourselves in helping to destroy them.

Jesus' teachings are also reduced by ignoring the central question, "Is this how God calls us to live?" We ask instead the secondary question, "Would our religious freedom, our church, or our Christian nation be destroyed if we lived like this?"

The Jewish leaders of Jesus' day made the same mistake. They met and discussed the impact of Jesus' miracles and teachings. They said, "If we let him go on like this, everyone will believe in him, and then the Romans will come and take away both our place [temple] and our nation" (John 11:48). Caiaphas went on to say that it would be better for one man to die than for the whole nation to be destroyed. There was no discussion of the validity of Jesus' teaching or the reality of his miracles. The Jewish leaders didn't even try to answer the central question, "Is this from God?" Instead, they too were asking the secondary question, "Will our positions and our worship and our nation be destroyed if we accept this Jesus?"

Jesus' teachings are also reduced by commonly held beliefs such as: "Well, you can't just let people walk over you" and "We have to stand up for our rights." These beliefs have been held and repeated for so long that we actually filter our understanding of the Bible through them. If our interpretation seems to be contrary to these beliefs, then we assume that of course Jesus meant something else. However, Jesus' teaching, life, and death do not demonstrate these commonly held beliefs as we usually mean them. When people say we must stand up for our rights or not let people run over us, they usually mean that if necessary we must use force to accomplish that purpose.

## Yielding from Strength

Jesus was never "run over." Even while they were killing him, he was in control. His life was not taken from him; he laid it down. His "posture" was not getting down so people could wipe their shoes on him; it was getting down to wipe their feet for them. He could not be put down because he knew who he was, and whose he was. The only "right" he claimed was the right—even the privilege—of doing the will of the Father. He didn't have to protect that right, because no one could take it from him.

According to Ronald J. Sider, in his book *Christ and Violence,* "The cross is the ultimate demonstration that God deals with His enemies through suffering love."[2] The cross was God's demonstration that he loves sinners. The cross is central to Jesus' command to love our enemies. We are not called to love our enemies as some new kind of law, but rather because the cross demonstrates that God loves them. Those who claim to follow Christ and fail to treat their enemies through suffering love, also fail to understand the atonement. They fail to understand the full purpose of the incarnation—the Word becoming flesh.

The New Testament clearly teaches that Christ came to reveal the full righteousness of God, which is the *same* righteousness to which he calls us. Jesus said, "Be perfect, therefore, as your heavenly Father is perfect." (Matthew 5:48). This statement directly followed his teaching to treat our enemies with love. Paul repeats this idea in Philippians 2:5-8, where he tells us to have the same attitude as Christ, who took a servant position and humbled himself and became obedient to death—even death on a cross!

## The Way of the Cross

Remember the old hymn?

> Must Jesus bear the cross alone,
> And all the world go free?
> No, there's a cross for ev'ryone,
> And there's a cross for me.

I had the privilege of hearing the bishop of Uganda speak. He had fled Uganda during the time the maniacal dictator, Idi Amin, was ruthlessly murdering hundreds of Christians—particularly Christian leaders. The oppressed church in Uganda saw much more clearly than do most American churches that the way of the cross is central to following Christ.

The New Testament clearly calls us not only to follow the teachings of Jesus, but also to follow him in suffering: "If anyone would come after me, he must deny himself and take up his cross and follow me" (Matthew 16:24). The cross is not just something Jesus did for us and now it's done. Peter writes:

> If you suffer for doing good and you endure it, this is commendable before God. To this you were called, because Christ suffered for you, leaving you an example, that you should follow in his steps. 1 Peter 2:20-21.

The rest of Peter's epistle continues to reflect not only that we are blessed if we suffer for doing good; but more importantly, it emphasizes that through this suffering there is power—power that overcomes evil. The early church experienced this power, first in the resurrection of Christ, again at Pentecost, and then—in spite of persecution—in the explosive growth of a whole new community of Jews and Gentiles. Not only were they fearless in the face of persecution; they were filled with joy!

## Our Comforter

The fearless joy of the early church can only be explained by the presence of the Holy Spirit among them. Jesus had told his followers to expect the world to hate them. He added, "No servant is greater than his master. If they persecuted me, they will persecute you also" (John 15:20). But Jesus also assured his followers, "I will ask the Father, and he will give you another

Counselor to be with you forever—the Spirit of truth. The world cannot accept him, because it neither sees him nor knows him. But you know him, for he lives with you and will be in you" (John 14:16-17).

"If anyone loves me, he will obey my teaching. My Father will love him, and we will come to him and make our home with him" (John 14:23). Further, Jesus said, "Peace I leave with you; my peace I give you. I do not give to you as the world gives. Do not let your hearts be troubled and do not be afraid" (John 14:27).

With such a promise, who *could* fear? Like Peter, we are stirred to declare, "I would die for you!" Jesus asks sadly, "Would you?" And we who were to be the children of God, citizens of the New Jerusalem, the kingdom of peace restored to the whole earth—we who were to be the followers to death, the forerunners of God's kingdom, the shape of things to come—we hear Jesus' words to Peter. They are rebuking words. "Put away your sword. All who take the sword, will perish by the sword."

Peter fully intended to prove his willingness to die for Jesus, but he obviously meant he would die fighting! He was not yet ready to follow Jesus in submitting to death. Like Peter, we have tried to defend the Christ—the Lord of the universe—with worldly weapons. We have cherished the badly mistaken notion that with Peter's bloody sword we could make a secure place in the world for the Christian church, the body of Christ, the forerunner of Christ's peaceful kingdom. It has been a false hope, and the church has badly compromised the central message of the gospel—the message of love.

The way to which Jesus calls us has seemed so difficult that we are tempted to postpone it until the millennium of Christ. We limit it to our personal relationships or call it an impossible ideal. But too many

Christians have followed that path for us to call it impossible. As we have seen, Jesus placed his teachings and his life in the middle of the sociopolitical situation of his time. He expected his disciples to follow.

## The Big Picture

It is sometimes said that Jesus' response to his enemies is not meant to be our example today, for he was looking at the greater picture and not just the immediate political situation of Israel at that time. But we also must realize that we fit into a greater picture of God at work in the world. As Christians, our only real hope for the world is in Christ's return to establish righteousness and justice once for all. It seems a paradox then that often we have strongly advocated the ways of war to preserve the imperfect governments of this age.

If we truly believe in the ultimate reality of God's kingdom, we needn't be so fearful and reluctant to risk our prestige, position, power, wealth, and even the happiness and comfort of our families in this imperfect age. Our witness to the world should be of Christ's redemptive, sacrificing love, which frees us from all fear, even the fear of death. The outcome, if we choose the way of suffering love, may seem like a defeat for righteousness and a victory for evil. We may suffer greatly. Yet we can walk through the valley of the shadow of death in the confidence that Christ has gone this way before to reconcile and evil world to himself.

# 5
## *War as the Lesser Evil*

The justification for war that I hear most often is that it is the lesser of two evils. Some say, "Certainly in an ideal world we wouldn't fight wars. Wars are evil. Of course they're wrong! But we have to live in the real world. And in the *real* world if good men don't stand up and fight, evil men will just take over."

### Nobody's Perfect

Some feel that since we can't live perfect lives in an imperfect world, we must simply accept God's forgiveness for our shortcomings. Indeed, we must continually accept God's forgiveness for our daily failures and even our periodic rebelliousness, but that is quite different from deliberately and consistently choosing and advocating a violent response in times of national danger that is counter to the teachings and example of Jesus. Again and again Christians have felt that they too must involve themselves in an evil business to prevent even greater evil from overtaking them. This sounds very much like the kind of reasoning used in "situation ethics."

## Making the Best of a Bad Situation

Situation ethics justifies what would generally be considered wrong, if a greater good will result. Thus, one might lie or steal to save a life. There is no absolute right or wrong, but rather in each situation each individual decides how to act to bring about the best results.

For example, the book *Situation Ethics* tells a story of a German woman held in a Russian detention camp just following World War II. The only way she could be released to return to her husband and two children (ages ten and twelve) was in the event that she became pregnant or too sick for the camp's medical capabilities. In these cases she would become a liability and therefore be returned to Germany. So she had a camp guard make her pregnant. Thus, she was able to leave, the family was happily reunited, and the baby was loved by the whole family as the cause of their reunion.[1]

We might ask whether adultery would be acceptable a second or third time for the sake of her family? If her children needed food and the only possible way she could raise money was through prostitution, would that be acceptable?

## What Are the Problems?

Critics of situation ethics do not argue that there are *no* times when one would judge a situation and decide, for example, to lie to save a life. The danger of situation ethics is just how quickly it can deteriorate into a mushy, aimless ethic: Do whatever feels right at the time.

At its best, situation ethics frees us from a strait-jacket of legalism. Love is our only guiding ethic. Jesus too was more concerned with being loving than with being legalistic.

At its worst, situation ethics says that there are no absolutes. Everything is relative. The center shifts; God slips from the picture. Humanism becomes *the* guiding principle of right and wrong. Francis Schaeffer defines humanism as man-centeredness. All reality and the meaning of life are defined in terms of human beings. With the person at the center we no longer have any assurance of a real God who is really active in our lives. We are left with only a concept of God expressed as "love" or "the greater good." With such a concept, God can disappear altogether, leaving us no solid ground for any absolute right or wrong—everything is relative.

Francis Schaeffer points to abortion as a primary example of this kind of ethics.[2] A mother's health, happiness, and freedom of choice take precedence over her baby's life. Also, with a population problem facing us, abortion becomes acceptable for "the greater good." But whose greater good—the mother's, the baby's, society's?

## War for "The Greater Good"

This type of situation ethics is also applied to war. Here too the guiding principle is man-centeredness. The chief consideration is "the greater good." Here again, we act as though there were no assurance of a real God personally involved in the redemption of the world. We have no assurance of a life beyond this one.

Most Christians' attitudes toward war have hardly differed at all from those of non-Christians. Schaeffer says the guiding principles for people today are personal peace and affluence.[3] These values have become so important to many Christians that they would willingly fight to keep or regain them. Our personal peace and affluence often become so important that we confuse them with freedom and justice.

Thus, when war is called necessary for "the greater good," we find that the greater good is our own freedom or affluence. Our greater good becomes more important than the lives of millions of Russian civilians, whose cities are targeted for destruction should their government sufficiently threaten that freedom and affluence. (Seldom in recent history have wars been fought between nations to actually defend people's lives. Most extermination or genocidal programs have been perpetrated internally by the government in power. Hitler was a notable exception in the case of the Jews.)

Not only is our freedom seen as more important for "the greater good" than *their* lives; our freedom is often seen as more important than our *own* lives. "Better dead than red" and "Give me liberty or give me death"— these declarations seem to exhibit an especially man-centered philosophy. To believe that life without political freedom is not worth living, denies the hope and freedom we have in Jesus Christ.

Immediately following Jesus' prediction that his followers would be hated and persecuted in the world, he prayed: "My prayer is not that you take them out of the world but that you protect them from the evil one" (John 17:15). Jesus was not asking that we be spared from suffering, but that we remain true to him.

### Christ—Our Center

Paul suffered all kinds of privation and persecution, yet he was able to glory in his weakness and suffering because they caused him to depend all the more on Christ's power. "That is why, for Christ's sake, I delight in weaknesses, in insults, in hardships, in persecutions, in difficulties. For when I am weak, then I am strong" (2 Corinthians 12:10). Our meaning in life as Christians is not defined in terms of what the world gives to or takes from us.

Some may say that communist and other totalitarian governments not only destroy freedom, but also try to completely wipe out belief in God. We have very little faith if we think evil men can wipe out the Christian gospel. The gospel of Jesus Christ has stood through countless persecutions and indeed is such a compelling message that it *flourishes* under persecution. Tertullian, one of the early Christian fathers, said, "The blood of the martyrs is seed for the church."

## Is Loving Enemies an Unchanging Ethic?

The situation ethics question in concrete terms would be this: Which is the greater evil—to go to war against Hitler or to allow him to overrun the world? If, however, we recognize that Christ's command to love is an unchanging ethic, then the question is rather: In the face of an evil threat shall we also be evil, or shall we obey Jesus, regardless? No matter how just a war may seem or how much we may wish to respond with force, Jesus calls us to absorb violence (like a shock absorber) rather than return it. In fact, we are to return love.

Absorbing violence seems so useless, so weak and inadequate, until we think seriously about the only alternative—upping the ante. We have raised the level of violence with every conflict and every threat. We have thought only of immediate advantage and temporary solutions, and failed to see where that leads us.

## Man's Inhumanity to Man

Richard Taylor, an advocate of Christian participation in war, says:

> It has seemed to me that a basic weakness in unqualified
> pacifism has been a sanguine view of human nature, with
> a failure to take with sufficient seriousness the depth of
> human depravity.[4]

On the contrary, if we take seriously enough the depth of human depravity, we will realize that evil and violence simply have no limit short of total self-destruction. This depravity is an important point and is the greatest flaw in the "lesser of evils" argument. The only alternative to the way of peace is to continue adding fuel to the destructive cycle of violence. To end one war, simply seems to prepare us for another. World War II is probably viewed as one of our most necessary wars. But the United States as victor ended the war by propelling us into the nuclear age. Now the specter of a nuclear holocaust far overshadows anything that Hitler did. The spiral of violence continues.

Many Christians feel that defeating Hitler was worth the cost in human life. The alternative would have been worse. But even though the results of World War II may seem to have improved our situation for now, yet because of our participation in escalating the violence, Christians have further compromised the central message of the gospel—love.

Our escalating capability for violence has actually changed the question of lesser evils. In a nuclear age there is no limit to evil and violence. No matter what the threat, the lesser evil is avoiding an all-out war. When we realize that a nuclear holocaust would be worse than *any* alternative, we can only trust God—as we always should have—to see to the outcome.

The fallacy of the "lesser of evils" argument is that Christians have thought they could participate in war and somehow contain or end the violence. Instead, they have only added to the violence. How much greater their impact would have been if Christians had always renounced the ways of a violent and evil world.

## God's War

As God's people, we *are* involved in a war against the forces of evil, but it is God's war—the war of the Lamb. He fights with a cross instead of a sword. (The next chapter will say more about the power of the cross.)

If we fight the forces of evil with their own methods, *evil is always the winner.* Evil will not only control our enemies; evil will control us.

But if we renounce violent retaliation, doesn't that mean we will simply have to accept defeat? It *would* be defeat in one sense if we fought for our nation and lost. But if we, God's people, resolve to put our trust in him alone and he allows our nation to be overthrown, that is not a defeat for his kingdom.

## What Does Jesus Expect?

We may still have questions about the consequences of *not* defeating a Hitler. Would Jesus expect us, for the sake of loving our enemies, to sacrifice our American way of life with its comfort, plenty, peacefulness, and fair play for a subhuman existence filled with suspicion and violence?

But does Jesus tell us to expect a life of comfort and plenty, peacefulness and fair play? No, exactly the opposite! So can we imagine Jesus encouraging us to take up arms to protect or attain such a life?

If we take up arms to keep evil and violent men from running over us, then we have misunderstood Jesus, who told us to take up our crosses and follow him. To take up arms is a direct refusal to take up the cross. We cannot carry both. When we follow Jesus, we should expect what he told us to expect: "No servant is greater than his master. If they persecuted me, they will persecute you also" (John 15:20).

Jesus knew his message would be threatening and that his followers wouldn't be very popular. Accordingly, it's difficult to imagine that he expected his followers to become wealthy, respected, and unpersecuted. I cannot conceive that he would expect us to fight to maintain such a status.

So if we ask whether it is better to respond with violence in a violent world or to sacrifice our lives for peace, we must ask: Better for what? If we mean better for our power, security, and wealth, the answer is often on the side of violence. If we mean better for demonstrating Christ's self-sacrificing love to a world full of hatred and violence, then there can be only one answer. To answer otherwise is not just a less-than-perfect choice; it is a failure to trust Jesus and the power of the cross. It is to lose faith that God will see us through and ultimately will set things right.

# 6

## *Trust in God vs. Common Sense*

We weren't expecting him when he came back,
And we were fighting;
He didn't ask, but we explained
That we'd have been, well...
Taken advantage of, overrun actually,
Maybe persecuted....
Still grasping for words,
He asked gently—for he knew our fear—
"Crucified, maybe?"

As the world stockpiles nuclear bomb on top of nuclear bomb, some Christians are shouting "Stop!" while others are shouting, "We need more!" Both want to avoid a devastating nuclear war, and each thinks the other is unrealistic.

All the various reasons for Christian participation in war stem from a desire to be realistic. Old Testament Israel had the same desire. We marvel at how quickly they would lose their trust in God. So soon after they were miraculously delivered from the mighty armies of Pharaoh without ever lifting a sword, they doubted whether they could go into Canaan with its scattered tribes. Even though God assured them that he would give the land to them, they chose to believe the ten spies who said they couldn't do it. They probably weren't consciously deciding to mistrust God, but rather were trying to realistically evaluate their situation.

David did the same thing when he took a census of Israel to see how many men he had who could be called to arms. The prophet Nathan took him to task for failing to trust God. David wasn't aiming to mistrust God; he just wanted to know how many men he had. But the prophet said if David trusted God, it wouldn't matter how many men he had. God doesn't depend on numbers.

## Faith Confronts Reality

The people of the Bible found that God had a way of changing what seemed like hard realities. Therefore, people of faith could look at their situation with a perspective different from that of their worldly neighbors. This fact contrasts with the pragmatic, "realistic" arguments for military strength of much of the church today. The church's arguments differ hardly at all from those of non-Christians.

We see our enemies bent on domination, opposed to freedom, and antichurch. The "hard reality" of an evil world tells us that if we aren't strong and prepared to fight, our way of life will be destroyed. "Common sense" seems to tell us that we must be prepared to defeat such enemies.

On the other hand, how can we seek to take the life of someone for whom Christ died, and still claim to follow Christ? We accept as part of our faith that God loves our enemies as much as us. He wants to redeem them too. But how does he intend for us to deal with them?

## He Sends Rain on the Just and the Unjust

Often the Old Testament writers leave the impression that God is only concerned about Israel (although some of the prophets speak of God's wider concern). Any such impression, however, is corrected in the New Testament, from which we learn of God's concern for all people—cvcn his cncmics. If we study the New Testament seriously, asking whether there is any indication there that it is God's will for us, his children, to take up arms and kill the enemies of justice and freedom and righteousness, how must we answer?

Vernard Eller says that once we see God's desire to redeem *all* people, we will realize that in an evil world *man is not the enemy.* But it's easy to lose sight of that fact. It seems we must fight those who oppose God's will and purpose.

> The logic is altogether correct, but what also is involved is a failure of *faith* in the capabilities of God. *As far as man can see,* the only alternatives are either to let the plan of God be frustrated or take out the obstructionists. And so he chooses what is obviously the least objectionable and most faithful alternative. . . .

> Yet on the other hand, if God's fight is *for the sake of man,* all men, then certainly he must have the wherewithal for getting us there without crunching some men, *any man,* in the process. This then is *faith,* true faith: to believe that God has ways of achieving his purpose without contradicting his purpose in the achieving of it—even when, from our position, we can't begin to imagine what those ways might be.[1]

Too often the church has expected God to triumph eventually (in one sudden burst of power), but in the meantime has felt we must be "realistic" and stomp our enemies before they take over the world. Indeed, we have shown very little trust in Jesus. Perhaps, like Jonah, we'd rather see our enemies crushed than saved.

God's love for his own enemies simply can't be fathomed. He draws *all* people to himself. We must make a choice to work toward God's goals and purposes or to put our own goals and purposes first. To choose war is rebellion against God's purposes and mistrust of God's judgment. It is sin. Of one thing we can be sure, we cannot bring God's redemption to sinful humanity by matching its methods—gun for gun, bomb for bomb.

## Faith as Obedience

How is it that so much of the church has not seen war as a sin in which Christians should not be involved? I believe the answer to that question is simple. The church has lacked faith in God's Word.

How can that be? Certainly evangelical churches have emphasized believing all of God's Word—creation, Jonah, the virgin birth, the resurrection, and even the more hazy details of Christ's return. We believe that all of God's Word is true! Yes and even literally true.

But at times we have taken belief in the doctrines and historical accuracy of the Bible to be the same as placing our trust in God—the Word. We have had belief but lacked the trust that leads to obedience. Trust is not some vague inner feeling; it is expressed in real and concrete ways.

As we learn from Hebrews 11, Abraham and all the other great heroes of faith were not heroes simply because they were able to believe the incredible. They were heroes of faith because they *acted* in obedience to God even when there was no visible assurance that their actions would "work" or be rewarded.

Jesus calls us to love our enemies and do good to those who hate us. If we really trust Jesus, we will treat our enemies the way he has instructed us to, without asking, "Is it safe?" or "Will it work?" or "When does it apply?" Enemies are to be shown love.

## Faith Confronts Fear

What if *all* Christians would say: "We will show love to all our enemies and no longer participate in a military defense which seeks to defeat and destroy our enemies"?

The first question that pops up is one of fear. "Yes, but then what would happen to us?"

Catherine Marshall, who has made some of the strongest contributions to my spiritual growth, defines fear as not believing that God can help in our situation. Fear is a lack of trust and needs to be treated like any other sin. We need to confess it and repent.

> Again and again we hear that cry of His, "O men how little you trust Him!" (Matt. 6:30). In the cry there is more than a little rebuke and sorrow along with a sort of marvelling astonishment that men could be so blind: "Why are you afraid? How little you trust God!" (Matt. 8:26). Behind Jesus' sharp reaction to our faithless fears lay His consistent viewpoint that this is our Father's world still in His control.[2]

If we believe that our Father is still in control, we know that he can be trusted to direct history as he sees fit. We don't need to fear that if we are obedient to his command to love our enemies, that somehow his purpose and will in the world will be thwarted. Indeed, as we try to save the world by force, we are acting counter to the very kingdom that God is establishing.

## False Security

We follow a different prince—the prince of peace. He said, "My kingdom is not of this world. If it were, my servants would fight" (John 18:36). And to Peter in the garden he said, "All who draw the sword will die by the sword" (Matthew 26:52). We are condemned to die by the very weapons we take up to protect ourselves. Today with our nuclear weapons, the truth of these words becomes more obvious than ever. Our nuclear warheads have not brought us the security we hoped for. As we frantically and madly continue building more and greater bombs, we only insure an even greater destruction for ourselves. The more we strive for security, the more doomed we become. This paradox, more than anything, reveals the satanic nature of the lies underlying the nuclear arms race.

## Saved by the Rapture?

Through their reading of prophecy some people believe that Christians need not fear a nuclear holocaust. The rapture will have removed them from the earth before this terrible tribulation comes. Like the early church, we should always maintain the expectant hope of Christ's return. But our record on using prophecy to accurately predict an event, *before* it happens is very poor indeed. After the event, the prophecies predicting it have seemed obvious. Who could foretell Hitler's holocaust, for example?

In any event, our confidence in prophecy should not induce us to continue in a disastrous and disobedient direction because we don't think we'll be around to suffer the consequences of our actions. To do so would directly contradict the purpose of the prophets, who nearly always included the following admonition in their message: In light of these coming events (or because the time is so short), be faithful and obedient to the very end.

## Forsaking All for Jesus

And if we are faithful? The worst that the evil forces can do will only draw us closer to Jesus, the source of our strength, or send us directly into his loving presence. Some may feel that they would be personally willing to suffer, but they couldn't stand to have their families or loved ones suffer. This tendency may be what Jesus was thinking of when he said we must love him more than home and family—not that we will always need to forsake home and family to follow him, but that following him may at times entail sacrificing the safety of our homes and our families.

Forsaking has another side too. If we are faithful to Christ's call to discipleship, then our families may forsake us. Jesus' primary persecution was not from Rome, the secular outsiders. It was from Israel, his own people, the religious insiders. In the same way, if many of us Christians are obedient in refusing to take up arms when the nation is threatened, then our friends and family and neighbors and government will begin to turn hostile and we will see a reduction of our religious freedoms.

## Freedom Ends Where "National Security" Begins

We have our present religious freedom because Christianity has usually not affected people's willingness to fight for the nation. (In recent wars so few Christians have refused to fight that they were no threat and thus were allowed exemption.) It is no wonder that our government continues to grant religious freedom to such a faithful, unthreatening ally as the church. Such freedom is not a reward from God for our faithfulness, as some imagine. It is the result of our compromising unfaithfulness.

The church in the "free world" has become complacent, comfortable, and self-preserving precisely because she has made her peace with the rulers of this age. You protect me; I'll bless your wars. The church has become totally confused about the true source of peace and security. Therefore, the church has grown fat—having sold her birthright for a bowl of pottage. Is it any wonder the church acts so much like the rest of the world?

We Christians have been like unfaithful Israel. When God wanted to give them the land, they usually ran ahead and did it their own way. Because of our "realistic" fears we, like Israel, have allied ourselves to the kingdoms of this world. Israel of old must have thought: "Sure, we should trust God, but we'll be even safer with a regular standing army and also with Egypt and all her horses and chariots on our side."

## Faith Outlasts Many Governments

We should not be overwhelmed, as Israel was, by the seeming invincibility of the evil forces surrounding us. As history has shown, the control exerted by worldly leaders over their people is a thin veneer, broken and patched many times. But underlying the veneer is often a strong, continuing, unshakable reservoir of faith that has outlasted many veneers. The church has remained strong in many communist countries in spite of the government's efforts to discourage Christianity. This is especially true in Poland.

When self-seeking worldly leaders struggle for control and power within their countries, it doesn't take much of a push from God for the whole government to unravel. We must never doubt that God has control of all our enemies.

## Will It Work?

Some pacifists believe nonviolence is an effective alternative to bring about change. They point to Gandhi and Martin Luther King to show that the nonviolent method can work. However, because of man's capacity for violence, we cannot suppose that if we laid down our arms, our enemies would necessarily begin to respond favorably. Hitler's armies eradicated nonviolent and violent Jews with equal unconcern. In other situations nonviolent action *has* been an effective method of political change. We can't advocate the way of peace because it always "works" or is "effective" in the short term. But it is the way to which Jesus calls us.

(I have purposely not made a strong distinction between the nonviolent use of power exercised by Gandhi and the nonresistant position in which coercion isn't used at all. A discussion of various alternatives to war is beyond the scope of this book.)

## *I Never Promised You a Rose Garden*

Other pacifists feel that if Christians had the faith to lay down their arms, then God would protect them from their enemies. He can and may do just that. But we must not expect that God will necessarily intervene to save us from the evil forces around us. Like the three Israelites who refused to bow to Nebuchadnezzar's golden image, we can say,

> The God we serve is able to save us. . . . But even if he does not, we want you to know, O king, that we will not serve your gods or worship the image of gold you have set up. Daniel 3:17-18.

We can't know what God will do if we step out in faith. God is God, and we are but his creation. We may lose home and family and possessions and even our lives. In fact, Jesus told his disciples to expect just that: "If you belonged to the world, it would love you as its own. As it is, you do not belong to the world, but I have chosen you out of the world. That is why the world hates you.'. .. No servant is greater than his master. If they persecuted me, they will persecute you also" (John 15:19-20). So we see that if we want to know how we'll be treated when we follow Christ, we need only look at how he was treated. But still we need not fear, for we know that whatever happens, Jesus will be there walking with us. His Holy Spirit will guide us, and nothing can touch us—nothing—unless he allows it.

We need not *seek* martyrdom in order to prove our faith. We cannot judge our faithfulness on the basis of whether we are suffering persecution, but only on the basis of God's Word as it reveals the kind of faithfulness to which Christ calls us.

Jesus did not seek martyrdom, but neither did he try to avoid it. Our primary Christian symbol, the cross, is a martyr's symbol. The early church accepted crossbearing as the Christian way of life. Jesus said that whoever wishes to follow him must first take up a cross.

Looking back on periods of martyrdom, the Christian church generally evaluates them as highlights in church history—not as times of weakness, but of strength. For Christ and the martyrs, the church accepts the cross as the way of obedience. The church does not say that Christ or the martyrs should have stood up for their rights or fought back (death with honor), or even fled.

The cross today is often the same as Paul said it was in his day—"a stumbling block" for the religious community and "foolishness" to the secular world (1 Corinthians 1:23).

In light of the cross, we see how false were our former presuppositions of how we must temper Jesus' teachings to the "real world." Many Christians say we must fight to defend our freedom to worship God, but Jesus never promised us that or any other political freedom. Jesus Christ is our freedom!

## Defeat Becomes Victory

Just as Jesus went before us to the cross, so he walks before us in the resurrection. If Jesus' work had ended at the cross, he might well have been forgotten; but God raised him up, and he now reigns as King of kings and Lord of lords.

From the ashes of defeat sprang a fire—the fire of Pentecost, God's sign of hope for a restored creation. While he had confused the people's tongues at Babel, on the day of Pentecost the crowds heard everything in their own languages. Babel was reversed! Christ broke down the wall. The good news is that we can be reconciled to God, who has seemed far from us. We can be reconciled to the fellow humans we have feared as enemies.

Because of the power of the Holy Spirit and the absolute assurance of the resurrection, Jesus' followers can speak and live boldly in the new reality—even in the face of enemies. The resurrection assures us that the victory is won already. That is why we can afford the costly way of nonviolence. With Jesus Christ going before us we walk in the glorious light of his resurrection.

## What Is the New Reality?

The reality of the cross and the resurrection is that Jesus unmasked the powers and showed they had no power at all. He said, "All authority in heaven and on earth has been given to me" (Matthew 28:18). This is the reality in which his followers are to operate.

In the order of his kingdom all struggles for power and control are irrelevant. Jesus told his disciples: "Those who are regarded as rulers [so-called rulers— Moffatt] of the Gentiles lord it over them, and their high officials exercise authority over them. Not so with you. Instead, whoever wants to become great among you must be your servant, and whoever wants to be first must be slave of all" (Mark 10:42-44). Jesus simply wasn't impressed with the rulers who thought they were in control. He said as much to Pilate, "You would have no power over me if it were not given to you from above" (John 19:11). Pilate thought he had the ultimate power over Jesus—the power of execution. Jesus marched to a different drummer; he fought a higher battle. Pilate had no idea.

## The REAL Battle

Jesus told his followers, "Do not be afraid of those who kill the body but cannot kill the soul. Rather, be afraid of the one who can destroy both soul and body in hell" (Matthew 10:28). I believe the church would have responded differently to war if they had understood what Jesus meant—and believed it. By taking a sword, the church puts itself on the wrong side of the *real* battle; Christians have fought the wrong kind of battle— often against other Christians, with whom they should have been joined in Christ.

A very real war is raging. Our actions for good or for evil determine which side we are fighting for. But it is spiritual warfare. The rulers of this age, according to Ephesians 6:12, are under the influence of evil spiritual forces. Man is not the enemy; Satan is. Guns might be effective if we were only fighting men, but they're totally ineffective against Satan. In taking up arms we play right into his hands. We are fighting his battle. "Our struggle is not against flesh and blood."

In 1 Corinthians 2:6-8, Paul says more about what the *real* situation is:

> We do, however, speak a message of wisdom among the mature, but not the wisdom of this age or of the rulers of this age, who are coming to nothing. No, we speak of God's

> secret wisdom, a wisdom that has been hidden and that
> God destined for our glory before time began. None of the
> rulers of this age understood it, for if they had, they would
> not have crucified the Lord of glory.

If the rulers of this age understood what is really happening, they would certainly not have killed the High King's Son, and they wouldn't go on killing each other. But we who are mature—we of the new birth—are supposed to have our eyes opened. We know what the *real* battle is. We should not be fooled by the great liar into fighting against the very people whom the King is fighting for.

Jesus faced the same hard realities of an evil world that we face today. The "troubled masses" surrounding him and even his own disciples kept pushing him toward a revolution. Oppressed people always yearn to be free. Some feel Judas had no intention of destroying Jesus; he simply wanted to force Christ's hand. Surely Jesus was tempted to take up a sword to throw off the oppressive weight of Roman rule.

What if Jesus *had* started a revolution? If he had succeeded in throwing Rome out of Palestine? If he had even overthrown Rome completely? Within a few years the power would have shifted again. Israel would have been no closer to following God than before. Rome and all the rest of us Gentiles would never have heard of the God of Israel. And Jesus would have been merely one more liberator as obscure as the Maccabees before him.

## Peace Through the Cross

Jesus knew all that. He didn't reject violent revolution because it was too dangerous, but because it was too weak. Since the human problem is spiritual, the sword never reaches its root; the way of the cross does. If only we could see as clearly today as Jesus did then.

Our response to human oppression should be the same as Christ's. Rather than seeking for justice and freedom and peace through fighting, we should be suffering alongside the oppressed—even at the risk of our lives. This kind of suffering love was displayed by the nuns and priests who were killed in El Salvador and Guatemala. These heroes of faith chose to keep working with the poor and oppressed even though they knew the political situation was very dangerous.

Does it seem idealistic, or unrealistic, to think Christians would willingly give their lives rather than fight? It shouldn't be any more idealistic for us to lose our lives for the cause of God's kingdom, than that millions have given their lives for imperfect, temporal kingdoms. It should be more reasonable to give one's life for peace nonviolently than violently.

Still, we feel so helpless and inadequate to do anything for those who are oppressed or for those we fear would oppress us. We profess great faith in the power of prayer, but our enemies seem so threatening. To say that at least we can pray, doesn't seem like much *until* we recognize the true nature of the struggle as spiritual; then prayer is everything.

## But What About Our Fears?

Let's return to the two camps of Christians mentioned at the beginning of the chapter. Some are shouting, "Stop nuclear arms!" and others are shouting, "More nuclear arms!" Both want to be realistic; often neither of them is. Both responses are often based on fear, rather than the ultimate reality that the cross and resurrection of Christ have destroyed the power of sin and death.

So to those who are simply seeking to be realistic—to those who would ask, "But what would happen to us if we all refused to defend ourselves?"—Jesus would say again, "Oh you of little faith!" He would offer this encouragement: "Take heart! I have overcome the world" (John 16:33)—not "shall overcome" or "am overcoming," but "*have* overcome!" And he would say, "Do not be afraid, little flock, for your Father has been pleased to give you the kingdom" (Luke 12:32).

A whole new reality has broken in on the world—the reality of God at work building his kingdom. All the struggles for power and wealth and security around us are struggles for things that are temporary and fleeting and uncertain. Living and working for that greater reality—the kingdom of God, which is already among us—is the only hope we have that is realistic and secure and final.

> Peace I leave with you;
> My peace I give you.
> I do not give to you as the world gives.
> Do not let your hearts be troubled
> And do not be afraid.    John 14:27.

# 7
## Submitting to Those in Authority

"To be a conscientious objector and not have to fight is a good deal for you so long as the government gives you a choice," someone once said to me. "But what if they didn't give you a choice? Then you'd *have* to fight like everybody else."

His mistake was in thinking the only choices we have are those the government gives us. There may be unpleasant consequences if we refuse any of the choices the government offers—but we always have a choice.

Many Christians advocate support for the military because Paul tells us to obey the government. This would be no argument at all for sincere, Bible-believing Christians if they became convinced that war is disobedience and rebellion against God. Peter said boldly, "We must obey God rather than men!" Staunch Christian people have always said the same when they felt that human institutions or authorities were asking them to disobey God. The heart of the issue is not whether we should or shouldn't be obedient to the government. The only real issue for Christians is whether or not the government is asking us to do something against God's will. The church must reexamine how honestly it has applied the Bible to the question of whether war is within God's will.

## An Agent of Justice

Romans 13:1-4 is used most often to show that the use of the sword *is* within God's will. This passage should not be used as it often is to support blind obedience to the government. But we can ask, "Do these verses support participation in war as a part of the God-given order?"

> Everyone must submit himself to the governing authorities, for there is no authority except that which God has established.... Consequently, he who rebels against the authority is rebelling against what God has instituted, and those who do so will bring judgment on themselves. For rulers hold no terror for those who do right, but for those who do wrong. Do you want to be free from fear of the one in authority? Then do what is right and he will commend you. For he is God's servant to do you good. But if you do wrong, be afraid, for he does not bear the sword for nothing. He is God's servant, an agent of wrath to bring punishment on the wrongdoer.

It is important to note that the government Paul was writing about was a police-state occupation. Even though he says worldly governments are ordained of God, he doesn't confuse them with God's kingdom or say that they are obedient to God's will. The point he is making is not at all that Christians will participate in the government's ruling function, but only that they should not rebel against it. He does not say Christians will help to bear the sword, but only assures the Christians at Rome that if they behave themselves, the government won't use the sword against them. When Paul wrote this epistle, the Roman government had not yet begun its worst persecution of Christians, nor had they begun demanding emperor worship. Writing the book of Revelation after these persecutions had begun, the apostle John certainly had a less positive view of the Roman government of his day.

To simply take what Paul says out of his context and to apply it to any political situation would be overly optimistic, especially since he says, "Rulers hold no terror for those who do right.... Do what is right and [the one in authority] will commend you. For he is God's servant to do you good." Paul isn't saying, "Do whatever the government asks because whatever it asks is God's will." History is abundantly clear in refuting that. Christians in Hitler's Germany, for example, could not have easily applied this passage to their government. They knew all too well that doing right would often bring severe punishment and even death.

## Is War like Police Work?

Of course, that still doesn't quite answer the question of the Christian's participation in the "punishing" function of a government not gone berserk, but on the side of justice.

Paul was not writing in this letter about the government's function of waging war; he was writing about their police function. Thus, the only bearing this passage has on the question of war arises from whatever parallels can be drawn between controlling burglars, snipers, or rioters and declaring war on a nation that threatens our national, economic, or political security.

There are clear differences between police action and war. One difference is the greater regard in police work for the uninvolved and bystanders. If the police used war methods, they might bomb the building where a sniper is hiding, even though others are in the building. Another difference is that usually the criminal's acts are not motivated by ideological reasons whereby he feels his actions are right and just. Opposing Christian nations have both prayed that God give their side the victory. Criminals probably don't pray that their crimes will succeed. In general, the question of who is right and who is wrong is usually clearer and more universally agreed upon in police work than it is in war. A final difference between police and soldiers is the attitude with which they are trained to function. Police are trained to exercise a high degree of self-control and careful judgment—to be unruled by emotions. Soldiers, on the other hand, are trained to hate—to be killers.

## How Can We Keep Order?

There are also parallels between police functions and fighting wars. Here I must admit to some ambiguity in my own position on the question of how we are to keep order in society. There is an obvious weakness in claiming that wars are fought to keep international order. If we *had* to fight to stop Hitler, why didn't we fight to stop Idi Amin? Nevertheless, in spite of most wars being fought to gain or protect wealth, power, influence, "turf," and other "vital interests," they are usually *portrayed* as keeping international order.

I can give an answer to the question of keeping order. It isn't that pacifists are more irresponsible, as is often claimed, but that they are more willing to be vulnerable. I'm not sure that answer is entirely satisfactory, however.

So if I accept pacifism, I have some problems about how to keep order in society. But if I reject pacifism, I have the problem of what to do with Jesus. Jesus seems to smile and say: "I didn't leave you in charge of figuring out how to order the world anyway. I left you to be a light. Follow me."

## Did Paul Include National Defense?

Whatever conclusion we reach concerning the use of police force (and I don't have a conclusion), there are still significant differences in both the methods and purposes of civil order and warfare. In light of these differences, I do not think Romans 13 should be expanded beyond its own context of police functions to cover military defense as well.

To test this interpretation, let's try to imagine how Paul would have responded if Rome had been threatened by Egypt, Syria, or, as later on, by the barbarians. Would he have said Rome was ordained of God to keep out the invaders? I don't think so. Rather, he would probably have said the invaders were ordained of God to bring judgment on Rome. An example of this perspective is the way the prophets spoke of Babylon, which came to be known as the very epitome or symbol of evil. Yet several biblical writers depicted Babylon as the agent of God, even as they threatened Israel and later took the Israelites into captivity (e.g., Ezekiel 21). Jeremiah advised submitting to Babylon's invasion, rather than fighting, because this was God's judgment. So we see that even evil forces have been portrayed as agents ordained by God.

The prophets could depict Babylon as God's punishing agent against a disobedient Israel, not advocating Israel's involvement with Babylon, but only submission to her. In the same way, Paul can depict the "governing authorities" as God's punishing agent against the wicked, not advocating Christian participation in the government's action, but only submission to the government.

## Overcome Evil with Good

The last several verses of Romans 12 give us some perspective on Paul's attitude toward governing authorities in the first verses of Romans 13. These verses especially raise doubts that the Romans 13 passage can be used to support Christian participation in wars.

> Do not repay anyone evil for evil. Be careful to do what is right in the eyes of everybody. If it is possible, as far as it depends on you, live at peace with everyone. Do not take revenge, my friends, but leave room for God's wrath, for it is written: "It is mine to avenge; I will repay," says the Lord. On the contrary: "If your enemy is hungry, feed him; if he is thirsty, give him something to drink. In doing this, you will heap burning coals on his head." Do not be overcome by evil, but overcome evil with good. Romans 12:17-21.

The last verse is immediately followed by (remember, Paul didn't write his letters with chapters and verses): "Everyone must submit himself to the governing authorities" (Romans 13:1). In Romans 13, Paul was discouraging Christians from involvement with the various groups fighting for freedom from Roman tyranny. He was not interested in struggles for worldly power or control, or even freedom. His freedom was in Jesus Christ alone. This passage in Romans says more *against* Christian involvement in the Revolutionary War, for example, than in support of involvement in national defense.

The Christian way to relate to all human authority, good or evil (1 Peter 2:18), is through submission—the way of the cross. Peter calls for the same attitude of submission to authority that Paul does:

> Submit yourselves for the Lord's sake to every authority instituted among men: whether to the king, as the

supreme authority, or to governors, who are sent by him to punish those who do wrong and to commend those who do right. For it is God's will that by doing good you should silence the ignorant talk of foolish men. Live as free men, but do not use your freedom as a cover-up for evil; live as servants of God. Show proper respect to everyone: Love the brotherhood of believers, fear God, honor the king. Slaves, submit yourselves to your masters with all respect, not only to those who are good and considerate, but also to those who are harsh. 1 Peter 2:13-18.

Peter goes on to say that suffering for doing good is what Christ has called us to.

## A Word to Fellow Pacifists

I think I should step aside here briefly to add a word to some of my fellow pacifists. I believe these verses speak to the more militant pacifists: ". . . by doing good you should silence the ignorant talk of foolish men. . . . Do not use your freedom as a cover-up for evil. . . . Show proper respect to everyone." I'm not referring to marches, demonstrations, and prayer vigils which are an integral part of expressing opinions publicly in a democracy. I'm referring to those pacifists who are trespassing, breaking and entering, and vandalizing government property in a desperate attempt to be prophetic in an increasingly dangerous and evil world.

Some would liken such actions to Jesus' "illegal" cleansing of the temple. There are certain parallels. However, I don't believe Jesus just *happened* to pick the temple for cleansing instead of the Roman garrison. Certainly the violence of the Romans was a greater moral concern than the cheating of the temple money changers.

I'm not sure how we should apply Jesus' actions to our situation. I don't believe we have to make some literal application of doing exactly what Jesus did. But I really believe if Jesus were here today he would more quickly attack the churches for supporting violent and oppressive policies, than the military for conducting those policies.

We can't expect always to agree on what kinds of civil disobedience are appropriate. I think anyone who sees the Boston tea party as a proper form of protest should *not* be morally indignant with those who destroy military property to protest military policies. The issue of human life is a far higher moral concern than a tax on tea!

Most Christians would agree we have a moral obligation to practice civil disobedience when the government requires us to do anything contrary to the will of God. This is different from the civil disobedience for the sake of confrontation or protest.

My own concerns about destructive and disruptive protests is that we not compromise our message of peace by even *appearing* unpeaceful. I am also concerned that we not use our freedom in Christ in a way that brings discredit to our Christian witness. It is certainly true that our obedience to God's higher authority takes precedence over the sovereignty of all worldly governments. It is also true that whatever is entered or broken belongs first of all to the higher authority. Nevertheless, I believe Peter has something to say about militant protests, particularly in his words, ". . . by doing good you should silence the ignorant talk of foolish men," and his admonition, "Show proper respect to everyone."

## Submission Is Not Allegiance

In all these passages on our relationship to authorities, we are called to show honor, respect, and submission. We are not called to give obedience, allegiance, or loyalty to the government; our loyalty belongs to Christ. For the early Jewish Christians, the patriotic or nationalistic thing to do would have been to start a revolution. This is precisely what Paul and Peter and Jesus before that were telling them *not* to do.

Just as the admonition for slaves to submit to their masters is not a defense of slavery, neither is Peter's instruction to submit to government authorities a defense of nationalism and national defense. Both must be understood in light of the overall New Testament emphasis that God loves everyone equally—slaves, freemen, saints and sinners, and that Christ calls us to love our enemies and to be peacemakers.

The generally accepted method of interpreting the Bible is to take the plain and oft repeated concepts and use them to interpret passages which are more liable to a variety of interpretations. Out of fear for our own safety or even our existence, the church has inferred justifications for going to war against our enemies from Romans 13:1-4. As a result, Jesus' oft repeated and plain teachings to do good to our enemies, to accept rather than return violence, and to trust our heavenly Father to see us through, have been made to conform to the already accepted assumption that Christians are justified in participating in war.

Instead, if we believe that Christ is the central figure of divine revelation, we should accept his teaching and example as our touchstone from which to interpret Romans 13 and all the rest of Scripture. "For no one can lay any foundation other than the one already laid, which is Jesus Christ" (1 Corinthians 3:11).

## We Live in Two Kingdoms

We should still look at Romans 13 as it relates to the idea that Christians live in two legitimate kingdoms and can give full allegiance to both. These verses are often used in discussions of the two kingdoms concept. First there is the national, political, earthly kingdom; and second, the personal, spiritual, heavenly kingdom. Both are ordained by God, but each operates with different methods. The political kingdom, according to this line of thought, cannot realistically be expected to follow the ways of the spiritual kingdom. Many Christians argue that as members of both kingdoms we are to be obedient to each in its own sphere. For proof they may quote, "Give to Caesar what is Caesar's, and to God what is God's" (Matthew 22:21).

According to this concept, much of Jesus' teaching falls into the category of personal, spiritual teaching. Thus, "Love your enemies," although a principle of personal conduct, is not applied to the conduct of nations. Nations are not considered responsible for following the way of the cross. That is not to say that nations cannot be called to repentance or challenged to act justly. The call to follow the way of the cross, however, is limited primarily to individuals. Nations, on the other hand, have a legitimate right to bear the sword to keep peace within and without. As members of both the spiritual and the earthly kingdom, it is felt, we can rightly use violence against national enemies, but on a personal level we should be forgiving and loving toward our enemies.

## Can We Live Two Ethics?

Even if we believe that nations and individuals are ruled by different ethics, it does not follow that we can separate our own actions into categories of what we are doing personally and what we are doing nationally. If this were so, we could hide behind institutions for all kinds of sins. For example, some concerned Christians are coming to realize increasingly their *personal* responsibility for immoral business practices of companies in which they own stock.

We do live in two kingdoms—the temporal kingdom of this world and the kingdom of God—but we can only give primary allegiance to one. "You cannot serve two masters." There is no biblical basis for living a split ethic, with one set of rules for one kingdom and another set for the other. Such a method is a human invention for resolving the tension between Jesus and the use of violence so that neither needs to be renounced. In all other areas—political, economic, personal—the church has taught Christians to live a higher ethic.

## Church and State

The concept of separation of church and state is that the government shall not control the church and the church shall not control the government. Many have wrongly interpreted this to mean that the church is our guide in spiritual matters and the government in secular matters. If kings and rulers saw Christianity as a solely spiritual and inner experience not affecting political allegiance, there would be no reason for persecution. Governments have persecuted Christians precisely because they have felt a threat to their sovereignty.

Christians were not thrown to the lions because their Christianity made them more honest, gentle, and fair. They were thrown to the lions because they refused to give first allegiance to Caesar. In Rome no distinction was made between worship and allegiance. Today by neatly dividing worship and allegiance, the church is accepted *in its proper realm.* The state, however, goes right on claiming our allegiance in many areas of ultimate importance—matters of life and death and justice.

The reason finally that Pilate couldn't let Jesus go was that Jesus said to him, "You have no power over me." In essence he told Pilate, "Your power is irrelevant to what is really happening. I belong to another kingdom. My Father has my final allegiance, and the only power you have is what *he* allows you."

The gospel of peace, as the churches in America have experienced it and preached it, is no threat to the established order. Most of the churches have said, "Our political involvement will not hinder or discourage America's power and authority." In fact, many churches are openly committed to increasing the power and arms of the United States.

## Democracy Doesn't Insure Morality

Some Christians say they don't agree with war, but if their country called them, they feel they should go. Nowhere do we find biblical support for doing what we think is wrong simply because the majority thinks it is right. Somehow we've gotten the idea that the rule of the majority is a Christian concept. Jesus, on the other hand, assumed that Christians would be a minority, and indeed we are. We may at times influence the majority, but we never control them. We must beware that they don't control us. Rather than accepting the will of the majority when we don't agree on a moral issue, Christians should live out their minority convictions and accept whatever consequences society imposes on them.

Does this mean that the functions of the government are to be carried out only by non-Christians and that Christians should only be involved in the spiritual kingdom? No, Christians may involve themselves in the government, but only in those methods of the government that do not run counter to the teachings of Jesus.

In many areas of government, I'm sure, Christians have contributed to a higher moral standard of honesty, decency, and compassion. But nothing moral is gained by having Christians help to legislate and implement non-Christian actions.

Christ calls his followers to renounce violence. The result may well mean a cross. Just because we are citizens of the state and it refuses the way of the cross and chooses violence instead, does not mean that we are obligated to use its method. We know this way cannot bring real peace at all.

It may be that the violence of the state will even save us at times from suffering. The state expects us to be grateful, but we should not want to be saved by someone else's use of violence. Rather, we should say, as Jesus said to Peter when Peter was determined to protect him, "Put away your sword."

## Shouldn't We Defend the Weak?

This discussion can be carried a step further. Not only does the Christian pacifist refuse to participate in his own defense, but also the armed defense of the poor, the weak, and the innocent. Some may say that our refusal to defend the weak and innocent is participation in violence as truly as armed defense is; the refusal to fight for justice is to participate in injustice. We don't live in the world as it *ought* to be, they would contend, but must demonstrate love in the world *as it is*.[1]

Such a standard of justice seems persuasive until we set it alongside Jesus' example. Can we say that Jesus' refusal to fight to free the weak and oppressed people of Israel from the tyranny of Rome was somehow participation in that tyranny? Hardly. Did his refusal to fight to establish justice for Israel make him a collaborator in the injustices they suffered? Certainly not.

If Jesus had freed Israel from the injustices of Rome through violence, the result would have been temporary at best. In the same way, we must stop yielding to the temptation to go for the quick (but temporary) solutions of violence. As Jesus rode into Jerusalem, he wept for its inhabitants because they were without a leader and because he knew the destruction that would come to the city. He cried, "If only you had known today the way to peace" (Luke 19:42 paraphrased). But his empathy for their plight did not cause him to forsake the ways of God's kingdom.

As followers of Christ we should also weep for those who suffer under tyranny, but it would be futile to adopt ways contrary to God's kingdom in the hope of establishing peace and justice. If God can be long-suffering toward his enemies, we should be the same. If he can be patient in his work in the world, we should wait patiently for that day when we all can shout, "The kingdom of the world has become the kingdom of our Lord and of his Christ" (Revelation 11:15).

# 8
## *Our National Honor*

A military officer appeared on a Sunday morning television program to give his testimony for the Lord. He said that he was getting ready to return for his fourth term in Vietnam. As I remember, he had been much decorated. He spoke of how Jesus was so near to him in times of grave danger and how much Jesus meant to him while surrounded by soldiers who were turning to drugs, drink, and other sins. Then he told of his personal concern for the people of Vietnam—even the Vietcong. He recalled an occasion when they had just finished battle in one village and the dead were lying all about. As he looked at all those pitiful corpses, he was forced to wonder whether they had been prepared to meet the Lord. He sounded as though he really did care for the souls of people he had just helped to kill!

For centuries churches have lived with the paradox of belief in Christ and support of war. They have dismissed all those who question their position as radicals, subversives, and even atheists. Today in America the questioners are often respected as sincere, somewhat idealistic, fellow Christians. At the same time, there is the implied feeling, "Since we respect your position as valid for you, you also should respect ours as valid for us."

However, war is not a matter of individual conscience such as the choice to remain celibate, or be a vegetarian, or do without television. Rather, it is an issue whose consequences profoundly affect society and the church—not just the individual making the choice. It is an issue of faith. Will we choose to destroy our enemies, or will we be faithful to Christ's way of sacrificial loving? Will we trust our heavenly Father to be our only security, or will we try to make a secure place for ourselves by force?

We cannot place the blame for Christian participation in war on individual soldiers. The soldier speaking on television was simply reflecting the church's failure to deal seriously enough with Jesus' words regarding our treatment of enemies.

Again, we need to follow Jesus' example. He pronounced judgment on religious institutions and false teaching, but lovingly accepted weak, failing individuals who could see their own failings and come to repentance. His words of judgment were directed at those leaders who were more intent on maintaining their position than on living lives that demonstrated obedience to the will of God, justice for the poor and oppressed, and kindness toward their fellow human beings—particularly sinners.

## Breaking with Tradition

Often the leaders of established religious institutions feel a threat to their traditions and authority when they are challenged with a different teaching. And often significant changes come about only as individuals respond to a new idea. For this reason I am especially encouraged by the number of church leaders who have broken with tradition to speak out against nuclear arms. Some speak against war altogether.

Father Zabelka, formerly the military chaplain for the Hiroshima and Nagasaki bomb squadrons, says now:

> Until the various churches within Christianity repent and begin to proclaim by word and deed what Jesus proclaimed in relation to violence and enemies, there is no hope for anything other than ever-escalating violence and destruction. Christians the world over should be taught that Christ's teaching to love their enemies is not optional.[1]

It is, of course, difficult to change a fundamental interpretation of Scripture when it affects our lives so deeply as does the issue of nonparticipation in the military. A comparable experience in American history is our struggle with the issue of slavery. Many evangelical church leaders gave a strong, fervent witness against slavery.

## War and Slavery—Related Issues

The church today does not struggle with the question of slavery. That issue is pretty much resolved in the church's mind. Yet there is as much or more biblical precedent for slavery as for participation in war. One could point out that there was no word of rebuke for the soldiers or centurions whom Jesus and Paul encountered. In fact, Peter accepted the centurion Cornelius as an equal brother in the church.

But just as truly, Paul accepted Philemon, a slave owner, as an equal brother and sent his runaway slave back to him. Elsewhere Paul exhorted slaves to be subservient to their masters. All this biblical evidence made good rebuttals for Southern slave owners. But Paul also sent a letter to Philemon asking him to accept his slave Onesimus as an equal brother in the church. Paul also wrote that in Christ there is no distinction between slave and freeman. The implications of that position undermine completely the dehumanizing aspects of slavery, and slavery itself as practiced 150 years ago. In the same way, Jesus' teaching to love our enemies, his insistence that his followers are not of this world, and his prediction that his followers would be hated as he had been—all these undermine the position that supports war in the defense of a government of this world.

Several other helpful points can be made with our comparison of the issues of slavery and war. Just as there were slave owners who were Christians, so there are soldiers who are Christians. The word of judgment is against the sin itself. Slavery is demeaning, dehumanizing, and exploitive; it is not compatible with the life to which Christ calls us. War is demeaning, unspeakably violent and cruel; it is in total opposition to the way of redemptive, ministering love to which Jesus calls us.

In the Civil War, Christian brother was fighting Christian brother (even blood brothers fought each other). Surely the same good result, without the bloodshed and alienation, could have been attained through prayer and Christian admonition and the quiet convicting work of the Holy Spirit. But how often the issues of economic and political security blind us to Christ's call to follow him.

Even before slavery was abolished, some Christian slaveowners freed their slaves, thus giving prophetic witness to the freedom that all men and women have in Christ. Surely such acts had a greater effect on their slaveholding neighbors than all the impassioned speeches in Congress urging the abolition of slavery. However good the intentions of the abolitionists, their impassioned, strident power struggles in the Congress helped to raise emotions to the feverish pitch that led to war. It is unfortunate that it took a devastating war to decide the issue of slavery and finally bring the church to resolve that issue. We can sincerely hope that it will not take a nuclear holocaust to decide the issue of war and bring the church to realize the completely evil, degenerate, and irredeemable nature of war.

## Dying for Freedom

It must seem strange to many Christians to think of war in these terms. They may always have thought of the heroic dimension of wars and battles. Those who have lost fathers, brothers, husbands, and boyfriends may wish to think of the supreme sacrifice made for them. However, I suspect that many in their hours of grief must have wondered whether the freedom gained or the honor saved was worth their numbing loss.

Am I really saying that Christians should not be willing to die for the defense of their country? In the movie *Patton*, as he was admonishing fresh troops, the general said, "I want you to remember that no bastard ever won a war by dying for his country; he won it by making the other poor, dumb bastard die for his country." If going to war were simply a matter of dying for the freedom of others, it would be heroic. But the purpose of war is defeating the enemy, which largely means killing more of them than they kill of us.

## Killing for Freedom

In human terms the choice boils down to this: If you were given a gun and the choice of killing a Russian family standing on the other side of a room or of taking your family and going to live in the Soviet Union, most likely you would choose the latter. You may not necessarily like that choice. In fact, the move would probably be extremely unpleasant, but to avoid it simply wouldn't be worth killing people. I admit that this is a crude way of describing the choice we have in war. But war is also a very crude way of settling differences.

Although the happiness and freedom of our families may be worth dying for, they are not worth killing for. Furthermore, few wars have made us any more happy or free because we fought them. Often whatever advantage is gained is only short-term. It is doubtful whether *any-thing* useful was accomplished by many wars.

## What Have Our Wars Gained?

Let me emphasize that the preceding several sentences and the following paragraphs are only my own political opinions concerning the effectiveness of war. You may disagree strongly with these opinions. But they do not at all affect the question of Christian participation in war. The issues I have raised do not hinge on whether the way of peace is effective in human political terms, but instead on whether we are being obedient to Jesus Christ.

Catherine Marshall, in her book *Something More*, says, "Criticism, protest, even open rebellion, some-times seem the only ways that essential change can come about. What about the American Revolution—surely there is an example of great good coming out of revolt? Or . . . is it?"

She recalls that during her college days she helped with the clerical work on a book by Phillip Davidson, *Propagandists of the American Revolution*. She was surprised at "the extent to which propagandists aided by the Liberty Boys deliberately whipped up the inflamed feelings that led to war with England." She adds:

> That the American colonies should have received a great deal more understanding and eventual independence is unassailable. The question is, were war, revolution, hatred, and bloodshed the best way to achieve needed goals?

> Two hundred years later may we still not be suffering the results in the American temperament? Perhaps the "good" revolution was not as harmless as we like to think.[2]

In light of the intense oppression in much of the world today, it seems almost laughable to think of the colonies being oppressed by British rule. Canadians, who never fought such a war, haven't suffered from a lack of freedom.

What did the rest of our wars accomplish? The War of 1812 would have been totally averted if there had been faster communication systems or if the government had exercised patience for a few more days. The Civil War left us with Reconstruction and carpetbaggers and, although slavery ended, a seething pot of racial hatred that still boils over periodically. Other lesser wars of that century were largely imperialistic ventures to grab land and power.

World War I ended with a treaty so vindictive that it opened the door to the Nazis. World War II saw us allied with one despotic government, Russia, to overthrow another, Germany. That fact has left many with the feeling that we simply postponed the evil day. It is doubtful that the Korean and Vietnamese Wars gained very much at all for the people of Korea and Vietnam, though it is certain they caused untold suffering. Those wars surely stirred up much bad feeling in the United States and again left us with the feeling that the evil day had simply been postponed.

So then what has been accomplished by our country's ten or so wars that we, as members of God's kingdom, should have involved ourselves in and supported?

## Military Propaganda

One reason our military tradition has seemed so honorable is the rhetoric used when talking about war. Every war is presented in the most positive light; the negative aspects are played down. Thus, our wars are always defensive, never offensive. We don't support war—everyone is against war. Rather, we are asked to support our country, our defense, our freedom—or on a more personal level, our "brave fighting men." (The latter always brings to mind the young man from next door—such a fine fellow serving his country.)

Only during popular wars like World War I and World War II have supporters spoken glowingly of killing the enemy. In our more recent wars one was more likely to hear talk of stopping the communist threat or defending the free world (which means those countries on our side). We could go on and on with such examples of "whitewashed sepulchers." One country's freedom fighter is another country's terrorist. The colonial soldiers in our own Revolutionary War were guerrilla fighters with less reason to fight than the people of many Latin American countries today whose governments have been propped up, or even installed, by the United States.

We Christians will view the war issue more honestly when we look past all the flowery rhetoric and all the double-talk. We should understand what is really meant when we hear "national security," "national honor," "free world," "preemptive strikes," "liberation," or whatever term is used to describe or justify military actions. We could then respond to the war issue, not by asking, "How can we insure our personal or national survival?" but "How does Christ call us to live in a world of conflict?"

# 9
## *The Real Test*

On January 8, 1956, Jim Elliot, Nate Saint, Ed McCully, Pete Fleming, and Roger Youderian were murdered. Their mission had been to take the gospel to the Auca Indians of Ecuador. They knew their mission was dangerous. Contrary to what is generally thought, they did not go in unarmed. Two of the missionaries were conscientious objectors and would not carry weapons; the others did. However, they had all agreed that they would not use their weapons to kill, but only to intimidate. Even if attacked, they would not kill their attackers. But their mission was snuffed out before it really began.

Or was it? Less than three years later, Betty Elliot and Rachel Saint, Jim's wife and Nate's sister, returned to these same Auca Indians. They not only proclaimed, but also powerfully demonstrated the gospel that empowered them to love those who killed their husband and brother.

The missionaries may have better expressed their true intentions if they had gone in unarmed altogether. But their willingness, even though they *were* armed, to lay down their lives rather than kill their attackers, and their relatives' readiness to forgive and actively reach out in love to the Aucas, laid the groundwork for a positive response to the gospel among this hostile tribe.

What would the outcome have been if these men had tried to kill their attackers? Even if they had succeeded and escaped with their lives, how different the outcome would have been. Their families would hardly have been able to return to start the mission work with these Indians. Their witness would have been destroyed.

Somehow we understand that missionaries would jeopardize their mission if they went into the jungle prepared to kill to protect themselves. However, in America in an area of high crime rates we seem to feel it is right to be armed to protect ourselves and our property.

## Ambassadors for Christ

As Christians we are all to be missionaries wherever we find ourselves. If we live in fear (either pragmatic or paranoid) that keeps us armed, we cannot help but hinder our witness to the good news of Jesus Christ. Unarmed, we may be left in a vulnerable position—like missionaries in the jungle. But it is hardly expecting too much that Christians should be just as willing to die for the principles of God's kingdom as worldly soldiers are for the principles of earthly kingdoms.

Far fewer people have died for God's kingdom than have died for earthly kingdoms. And when they die defenselessly, as did the five missionaries, the impact of their death is a thousandfold the impact of those who die fighting. Indeed, the compelling story of the death of an innocent, defenseless man is at the heart of the gospel message.

## What About Your Family?

Let's bring the issue of killing down to the personal level. The question is often raised, "What if your family were threatened? Wouldn't you do whatever was necessary—even killing—to save your family?"

In the first place the situation is highly hypothetical. Second, the analogy to war is not entirely correct. And third, Christians who truly expect to be with the Lord when they die need not be so fearful that they arm themselves and prepare to take other peoples' lives in order to save their own.

The chances of even being in a position to save one's family from a killer are quite remote. Trying to resist or apprehend a killer would probably *increase* the chances of one's whole family being killed. We might notice from news stories how seldom people with guns in their homes manage to stop a murderer. Compare that with how often we hear reports of children finding guns at home and killing themselves, or people cleaning their guns and shooting themselves; a homeowner thinks someone is breaking in and shoots a friend or the newspaper boy, or someone in a sudden fit of temper shoots a friend or relative. Then we might simply ask, "How wise is it to be armed and ready for a murderer in the first place?"

The analogy of war to outright self-defense is usually not a very good analogy. Usually the aggressor nation does not intend to wipe out the people of another nation. Often the war is to attain power, land, resources, or to eliminate a threat. Freedom and a good life may be at stake, but usually not our lives. With war, unlike personal self-defense, all kinds of emotion-laden and hard-to-grasp concepts such as freedom, democracy, and nationalism come into play. War is more often like killing a robber when you don't have theft insurance. Our possessions should not be so important to us that we would take another's life to keep them. Applied to war, we certainly shouldn't sacrifice the lives of our sons to protect our standard of living or our oil.

Finally, Christians are quick to say that we should be willing to die for our faith if necessary. We should accept death rather than be disobedient to Jesus' teachings. So why is it so preposterous or idealistic to say that we should accept death at the hands of an enemy rather than kill him—whom Jesus tells us to love? Jesus said, "He who saves his life, will lose it, and he who loses his life for my sake, will save it." (Matthew 10:39)

## What If We Were Attacked?

In peaceful times it isn't that hard to declare that war is wrong and Christians shouldn't participate. It isn't hard to maintain such a position during a Vietnam-type war. In retrospect we may even admit that Christians shouldn't have fought in our Revolutionary War against England, a war which gave us only a slightly different political system—a little better perhaps, but hardly worth thousands of lives.

But the difficult part is the logical conclusion of this position against military participation. In the case of foreign attack, should Christians really refuse to help in the defense of the country? The biblical answer, I believe, is yes. Just because the cost is high and because it goes so drastically against our human nature, is no reason to disobey Christ's call to be peacemakers. The military may define war as peacekeeping, but Christians are not to be deceived. Loving our enemies was Christ's serious intention, and he never pretended that following him would be cheap.

What does it mean to refuse to help in the defense of our country? To clarify the issue, let's rephrase the question in its starkest dimension. Another government wishes to decrease the power of our government or even take over our government and radically change our way of life. It sends its young men against us to achieve that purpose. Now the question in that situation: Should Christians refuse to help kill those young men or to help in attacking the other nation to destroy its cities and millions of people living there? Put in "real" terms, the biblical answer is much more obvious.

Obvious, perhaps, but no less difficult. The church today finds it difficult to change its beliefs and practices regarding national defense for two reasons.

## The Difficulty of Changing Directions

First is the problem mentioned earlier—our tradition. How can the church remain credible and suddenly pronounce something a sin which before it often considered a noble cause? To that I can only say that we are called to obedience as God continually opens to us new truths.

Perhaps now we can see just how deep the differences are between the kingdom of God and the kingdoms of the world.

Ever since Constantine gave official approval to Christianity, and his successors made it the state religion (and enforced it), Christians have held the hope that by the use of force they could make a safe place in the world for Christianity. But the evil forces outside our "Christian nation" grow continually stronger. And the evil forces *within* are rotting us like bad apples in a barrel. All around us we see the decay. Our violent ways have only sped, not slowed, the decay. Now we can see

(1980). Early Christian attitudes toward war, violence, and the state.

Kaufman, Donald D. *What Belongs to Caesar?* (1969). Basic arguments against voluntary payment of war taxes.

Lasserre, Jean. *War and the Gospel* (1962). An analysis of Scriptures related to the ethical problem of war.

Lind, Millard C. *Yahweh Is a Warrior* (1980). The theology of warfare in ancient Israel.

Ramseyer, Robert L. *Mission and the Peace Witness* (1979). Implications of the biblical peace testimony for the evangelizing mission of the church.

Trocmé, André. *Jesus and the Nonviolent Revolution* (1973). The social and political relevance of Jesus.

Yoder, John H. *Nevertheless* (1971). The varieties and shortcomings of Christian pacifism.

_____. *The Original Revolution* (1972). Essays on Christian Pacifism.

## For Easy Reading

Beachey, Duane. *Faith in a Nuclear Age* (1983). A Christian response to war.

Drescher, John M. *Why I Am a Conscientious Objector* (1982). A personal summary of basic issues for every Christian facing military involvements.

Eller, Vernard. *War and Peace from Genesis to Revelation* (1981). Explores peace as a consistent theme developing throughout the Old and New Testaments.

Kaufman, Donald D. *The Tax Dilemma: Praying for Peace, Paying for War* (1978). Biblical, historical, and practical considerations on the war tax issue.

Kraybill, Donald B. *Facing Nuclear War* (1982). A plea for Christian witness.

FUNDERBURG LIBRARY

MANCHESTER COLLEGE

WITHDRAWN
from
Funderburg Library

of t
stat
Miller, J
the
Mo
Miller, M
Res
con
with
Sider, Ro
reap
Steiner, S
No
writ
Wenger,
men

*For Chil*
Bauman,
Stor
Moore, R
nove
Chri
Ohio

Smucker, Barbara Claassen. *Henry's Red Sea* (1955).
The dramatic escape of 1,000 Russian Mennonites
from Berlin following World War II.

that the spiral of violence—gun for gun, bomb for bomb—has no limit until we destroy everything we are trying to save. Perhaps as we see the fallacy of trusting in military force, we can hear anew Christ's call to trust in him for our security.

The second problem in changing our violent ways is that we are already dangerously high on the spiral of violence. So our efforts to be peacemakers are especially dangerous—somewhat like trying to let go of the tiger's tail. The die is cast. The nations have placed themselves in eyeball-to-eyeball confrontation, and neither side dares to back down or appear weak.

The call to obedience is Jeremiah's "unpatriotic" call not to resist the advancing forces.

## A New Twist to an Old Problem

Most of what I have said so far would apply equally well to any country or any century. But in our day a new factor urgently compels us to refuse to participate in our military defense—the nuclear factor.

In today's "real world"—with not only the possibility of nuclear war, but (many are saying) its probability— the only reasonable answer is to refuse to fight. To think that nuclear aggression—no matter who fires first—would preserve, save, or protect anything is insane! If given the choice of nuclear holocaust or communist rule, reasonable people could not choose nuclear holocaust.

Christians would be gravely misplacing their values to promote a policy of "better dead than red." Christians already in communist countries certainly aren't seeking to die rather than remain alive in those countries.

So even the situation ethics question of lesser evils, because of the nuclear factor, must be answered with a *no* to war. Nuclear war would be the greater evil!

## *Peace Will Conquer*

But look where that takes us. The evil forces would prevail!

Not at all. Ultimately, we *know*, the evil forces will be conquered. As at the empty tomb, God always has a way of turning defeat into victory. We may not always see how, but it is the faith of the book of Revelations which sustains us—the slain Lamb triumphs.

God *will* have the victory; our only responsibility is to be obedient to his way.

> If anyone is to go into captivity, into captivity he will go. If anyone is to be killed with the sword, with the sword he will be killed. This calls for patient endurance and faithfulness on the part of the saints.    Revelation 13:10.

The way of peace will finally prevail, not on its own merits, but because Jesus is the Prince of Peace and the victory is his.

# 10
## War
## and the
## Christian Witness

A well-known radio preacher with a very effective ministry once conceded privately that he could find no biblical support for participation in war. But he said, if he were to preach such a message he would lose a large share of his listening audience and consequently lose the opportunity to share the gospel with them.

Keeping our convictions to ourselves would certainly be the easier path. But if Christians from a church that has supported its nation's wars for centuries become convinced that going to war is being unfaithful to the call of Christ, then for them the meaning of the gospel is changed. How can they share the gospel without sharing their new understanding of it? How can others also learn unless they are told?

This gospel of peace is no hindrance to the story of salvation. It recovers the integrity of the old teachings of loving our enemies, being peacemakers, being members of God's kingdom, taking up our crosses and forsaking worldly ambitions. To repent from sin is not to be sorry we're so human; it is to turn from our sinful (and, in this case, violent) ways.

"Pacifism might work," a friend once told me, "if everyone were a Christian." He was wrong, because the church has not taught that "accepting Christ" means accepting his *way* and leaving behind the ways of a violent world. So Christians have been just as militaristic as non-Christians.

The church loses credibility if being a Christian means little more than being a good citizen. The church grows weaker as it stands for less and less. We dare not temper the gospel so that no one will be offended or turned away. Many Christians truly want their Christianity to stand for something. They want to be recognized as changed people—people with different values. And above all they want to make the call of Christ first in their lives.

This gospel of peace could be a strong asset to our witness beyond our national boundaries. We can see the effect on the worldwide church that our past military policies have had. In both North America and Europe, by allying ourselves as Christians to our countries and participating in their military exploits, we have hindered the spread of the gospel. In many countries Christianity has come to be seen as a largely Western religion.

If the Christian church had always dissociated itself from its respective country's military exploits, it would have a much more legitimate claim to being above the geographical and political boundaries that divide the kingdoms of this world. We should look at what the church might have been had we not so easily allied ourselves to worldly governments. Imagine the potential of a church unencumbered with vested interests in anything but the cause of Jesus Christ.

## *"Peace" Can Be a Fightin' Word*

Having noted the positive effect of the peace stance, we must at the same time recognize the tremendous potential of the military issue for dividing the church. We must pray for the leading of God's Holy Spirit in raising the issue. Some would prefer to let the Holy Spirit do the convicting and leave the church out of it. Jesus said that when the Holy Spirit comes he will convict the world of sin. He also said the Holy Spirit would lead us into all truth.

Just as the church involves itself in the work of leading people to the truth, the church must also be involved in warning the world of sin. If the church leaves individual Christians to decide for themselves what is right for them, the direction of the church—in spite of a few discerning, sensitive people—will be the path of least resistance.

As Christians we have said we will forsake all to follow Christ. Most of our forsaking is not very hard and would certainly not constitute taking up a cross to follow Jesus. So when a true cross comes our way, let us bear it boldly. In this case, if we truly become convinced of the evil of war, the question is not *whether* we will proclaim it but *how*.

## *Accepting the Person and Confronting the Sin*

If war and the preparation for war are signs of unfaithfulness, how are we to relate with love and acceptance to the thousands of soldiers who are Christians and church members? With an issue so specific, how do we challenge them, as well as all other Christians, to faithfulness without making them and their families feel rejected? Jesus provides our example. To the woman taken in adultery, he said, "Go and sin no more." He definitely accepted the adulteress and would have no part in stone-throwing, yet he called her behavior sin and asked her to stop it.

The church has seldom lived up to Jesus' example. It has often left the impression that to call an action sin is also to reject those who practice the sin. The church has boldly proclaimed the evil of drunkenness and sexual immorality, but few Christians are accused of mingling with drunks and prostitutes as Jesus was. As a caring and loving church we must work together to keep relationships open and accepting, without minimizing the obedience to which Christ calls us.

The attitude Jesus demonstrated to soldiers was one of genuine love for them as persons. The centurion who came to ask that Jesus heal his servant evidently sensed in Jesus a concern that reached beyond all boundaries. Jesus didn't seem just to be engaged in the Middle Eastern custom of overblown complimenting when he said of the centurion, "I tell you, I have not found such great faith even in Israel." Jesus did not advocate even nonviolent forms of protest against occupation soldiers; rather, he advocated carrying a soldier's bags two miles instead of the one mile which soldiers could rightfully demand.

This attitude of acceptance cannot be automatically read to justify being a soldier. As we noted earlier, Jesus seemed equally well disposed toward prostitutes. He praised the faith of the sinful woman who anointed his feet. And those sitting near him said, "If this man were a prophet, he would know who is touching him and what kind of woman she is—that she is a sinner" (Luke 7:39). This woman also sensed in Jesus a concern that reached beyond all boundaries. Jesus accepted her, even though he did not approve of the life she was living.

A second observation concerning Jesus' attitude

toward soldiers is that his words were directed toward enemy soldiers. The Roman soldiers in Palestine were loved about as much as the British soldiers in the American colonies in 1776. That is the last example Americans have of occupation forces. We can, however, imagine the humiliation and fear of occupation by a foreign communist enemy. If that were to happen, we would undoubtedly see little of Jesus' kind of compassion for the communist soldier.

The only conclusion, then, which we can draw from Jesus' encounters with soldiers is that they, like any and all persons, must be treated with love and acceptance. There will be no easy way to accomplish that while we raise the challenge for Christians to stop participating in the military. As a first step, those who begin to catch a vision for peacemaking must share it. Then in a spirit of love and prayer and fellowship, we must work together to help others respond to the call of peacemaking.

## More than Token Response

War is a serious evil, and Christians should give more than a token response to the call to peacemaking. Christians in the military can be challenged to consider leaving their careers, to find jobs more in keeping with the life of service to which Christ calls us. This may seem like too great a sacrifice to ask of our friends in the military. We could compare it to Jesus' asking the rich young ruler to go sell *all* that he had, give it to the poor, and then come follow him. The rich young ruler must have been shocked at such a request. It was too much to ask of him, and he turned and walked away. Jesus was grieved because he loved the young man very much.

When we fully understand how totally war stands in

opposition to the gospel of love brought to us in Jesus Christ, then it is not too much to ask any Christian to leave the military. As the heavenly visitors asked Lot and his family to leave their homes in the doomed city of Sodom, so we can urge fellow Christians to leave the doomed war machine and seek the way of peace.

Other Christians should be supportive of their friends in military careers who consider leaving for other occupations. They should do all they can to ease whatever financial hardships are encountered if their fellow Christians choose to step out in faith from their secure jobs in the military. This should be more than just token assistance. In this way we can help to bear one another's burdens.

## Fear Shouldn't Stop Us

Just as we need not worry ourselves about what would happen to our nation if we were to obey Christ's call to be peacemakers, so also we needn't be fearful of the unpopularity our obedient response would reap for the church. Whatever the effect of our forsaking the ways of worldly warfare, violence, and power struggles, we can certainly trust a loving Father and the presence of his Holy Spirit to sustain us, strengthen us, and give us joy!

We the followers of Jesus Christ are to be the wave of the future—the foreshadowing of God's heavenly kingdom. All around us fearful people call for ever newer weapons, ever larger stockpiles, ever greater forces. They rely in vain on these destructive weapons for their security. Jesus said that those who take the sword will perish by the sword.

We can rely on Jesus, the creative force, for all the security we could ever need. That is the good news of the gospel, which we should share with all the world.

# 11
## *Peacemakers in a World of War*

For two years I worked as an orderly at the Oklahoma University Hospital as an alternative to military service. I met another young fellow also working there as a conscientious objector. One day I asked him, "What did you do before you were drafted and came here?"

"I was working at Honeywell," he answered.

"Doing what?"

"Testing bomb detonators," he replied.

I was dumbfounded. He could probably have joined the army with less destructive results.

The call to be peacemakers goes far beyond nonparticipation in war—as essential as that is. It extends to our work and our personal relationships, including the relationship with our enemies. However, I have purposely limited the focus of this book to the way Jesus and the New Testament relate to the issue of war, so that the point cannot be missed or passed off lightly with, "Well, at least on a personal level we should be peacemakers." Peacemaking is a way of life.

How should this life-style of peacemaking be fleshed out? This question must be answered by churches, study groups, prayer fellowships, conferences, or whatever other Christian groups choose to wrestle with the issue. We will not all come to the same conclusions. But whatever our peacemaking life-style, we should try to be consistent with Jesus Christ and his Word. Unlike the example of my friend at the hospital, our peacemaking life-style needs to be internally consistent. I would hope that other Christians' responses to peacemaking would not be so narrow.

## How Uninvolved Can We Be?

I personally feel that any job directly contributing to the function of the military is a contribution to war. To other Christians it may not be as apparent that this would include military medical jobs, military chaplain jobs, or military clerical jobs. If you fail to see how such jobs compromise peacemaking, a comparison with a related issue might be helpful. Christians opposed to abortion would usually feel they should not work in abortion clinics. Most would not work even as postoperative nurses, clinic counselors, or secretaries.

We can of course never claim total uninvolvement or complete purity regarding any of the evils of an imperfect world. Our degree of uninvolvement should never be used to punish, or act self-righteous toward, those who are more involved. I think, for example, that we have very real responsibilities for our veterans.

Just as there is a danger of self-righteousness and "pickiness" in a discussion of degrees of involvement, there is the opposite danger of trivializing the whole issue of involvement in war.

Some friends of mine with civilian jobs at Tinker Air

Force Base have told me, "Just the fact that we live in the United States makes us all participants in one degree or another in the war-making of our country, so it's a relative matter. How can one person say where he draws the line is better than where someone else does?"

To see the fallacy of this reasoning, we need only apply it to another situation. One could say we all participate to some degree in our society's exploitation of sex and therefore the whole issue is relative. Since we all see exploitive newspaper ads or TV programs, we shouldn't act so self-righteous about setting limits at not buying pornography or not being sexually promiscuous or wherever we draw the line.

The fact is that in many areas Christians do draw lines, and for good reasons. We admit that there are gray areas of involvement, but we shouldn't let those so cloud the issue that even the obviously black and white areas look gray. Although there may be differences in our peacemaking life-style, they should not distract us from a basic commitment as Christians to end our participation in war.

## Some Positive Steps

It is not enough just to ask what we *shouldn't* do; we must also ask what we can and *should* do to actively promote peace. But until Christians are convinced that war is a sin in which they can not participate, it is pointless to talk about being peace*makers.* What good is there in discussing positive things we can do to promote peace if as soon as a war starts we all join the fight? Only when we are convinced that war is not the Christian's alternative are we ready to search for ways to be peacemakers.

The main power of the peacemaker is in prayer. Prayer, like peacemaking, is not just a passive activity.

Since the real cause of human violence and war is a spiritual problem, prayer is our most powerful offense. The peacemaking church must strengthen its bonds as a community of believers—gathered together to pray, to worship, and to encourage and nurture one another in an ever deepening awareness of where repentance from violence and obedience to Christ lead us. Having gained strength through prayer and from one another, peacemakers can then begin to demonstrate in their lives the new social realities of God's kingdom. The Bible clearly teaches that right relationships with our fellow humans are both a result and a reliable indicator of our relationship with God.

## Living by Kingdom Values

War is spawned by greed, injustice, and a struggle for power. In contrast, Christians' lives should reflect generosity with all they possess, active involvement in the needs of the poor and the oppressed, and a willingness to serve in the lowest of jobs if that is where the needs are. One area where these Kingdom values should be clearly expressed is in the way Christians choose their jobs. Instead of asking what we like most to do and where we can get ahead the quickest, we should ask what human needs we can meet. Most people have several abilities they could cultivate.

For example, a young Christian man may be planning to become a chemist because he knows he can get a good job with a chemical firm. He may rightly claim that he will be able to witness to the people he works with and that with his good salary he can help support a youth program at an inner-city church in a poor neighborhood.

This young man may also have the ability to relate to and work with young people. If he asked instead what human needs he could best meet, he might become the youth activity director at the inner-city church in the poor neighborhood.

Though his pay would likely be lower, the latter choice would probably come closer to what Jesus meant in his parable of the talents. It would be better steward-ship. Stewards are caretakers of the master's resources; Christian stewards should most concern themselves with how their Master wants his resources to be used.

## The Christian and Wealth

War is not the only area in which many Christians have not fully come to terms with Jesus Christ. With the issue of wealth too, many Christians have taken the position nearest that of the world. Jesus' remark about how extremely difficult it is for a rich man to enter heaven has been rendered almost meaningless. And only a few "fools" would think of selling all they have and giving it to the poor and *then* going to follow Jesus.

To live as well as our means will allow (sometimes better), to reinvest profits to make more, and to reinvest again is the norm in the Christian church. We justify this by thanking God for his rich blessings to us, failing to realize that what we have is not ours only. Our wealth is entrusted to us for the Master's use. Often the "bless-ings" we thank God for are actually the fruits of our own greed.

## Disagreement on Method
## Doesn't Change Message

A great deal more could be said about living a life-style more in keeping with Kingdom values of justice and concern for the poor. Ron Sider's excellent book *Rich Christians in an Age of Hunger* deals in depth with what the Bible teaches concerning wealth. Some critics have said the book is too simplistic in some of its economic reccommendations. The specific economic applications may need more careful discussion and refinement. However, that doesn't change Jesus' basic teachings about wealth. The same is true of the issue of war. We may differ in our methods of peacemaking, but that doesn't change the basic message of peace.

For some, peacemaking may mean bringing a prophetic message to the government through demonstrations or marches. Others will point out that Jesus and the apostles didn't try to change Rome's military policies.

Some may oppose paying military taxes on the grounds that the military depends on money as well as personnel. Others will point out Jesus' statement, "Give to Caesar what is Caesar's." We need not reach agreement in these gray areas before we can respond to the basic issue of opposing war.

Our refusal to participate in the military and all our efforts to promote peace and goodwill probably will not stop war or even stop our nation's mad rush to maintain military superiority. Nor will changing to a life-style less bent on consumption, less "dog-eat-dog," and more directed at serving human needs usher in a just and generous society. But Christians who begin to reorder their lives in these ways will be able to speak with more integrity about the love of Christ to their neighbors across the street and in other nations.

## We Preach a Gospel of Peace

Beyond prayer, probably the single most important thing we can do as peacemakers is to make the message of peace and suffering love an integral part of our evangelistic proclamation of the good news of Jesus Christ. It is not surprising that the world is violent beyond belief; but it is to the shame of the church that Christians have participated in and escalated the violence.

We are not called to change the world, We are called to live truly changed lives and to proclaim to the world the transforming love of Jesus Christ. It isn't that living good lives will earn us our salvation. Jesus alone has already earned our salvation. Now he calls us to follow him—to repent from our old ways. Repentance means changing the direction of our lives and walking a new way.

Jesus said, "If anyone loves me, he will obey my teaching" (John 14:23). To confess that Jesus is Lord doesn't mean just believing something about his divinity. It means living a life in which Jesus is the Lord, a life which reflects Christ living in us. A life which is indeed a witness to the saving, transforming love of Jesus Christ, the Prince of Peace, and to the power and joy of the Holy Spirit!

# *Epilogue*

Ponder for a moment the aftermath of a major nuclear war.

• • •

An old man sits and stares numbly at the devastated world. His entire family has been killed. A thirteen-year-old girl who lived several houses away sits beside him. Her whole family was killed too. Several days have gone by since the bomb fell. Still the old man and the girl have stayed. They are waiting for someone to come down their street to help bury their families.

The girl draws absentmindedly with her finger in the thick dust that has settled on everything. "Why did it happen?" she asks.

"I don't know." The old man sighs and looks around. "I suppose neither we nor they could give up until we'd at least tried our biggest weapons."

"Neither of us? You mean—" She hadn't thought about it, but before she finishes the question she knows the answer, "You mean we used the same weapons on them?"

"Yup."

"Then we're no better than they are, are we?" the girl frowns. "Why did we have them?"

"Because we didn't want to be caught unprepared."

"Unprepared for what?"

The old man thinks awhile. "I don't guess I know anymore. At the time, we wanted to be prepared to defend ourselves. It doesn't look like we could have. The only thing we were preparing for was destruction."

"Didn't we know what would happen?"

"Yeah, we knew. They'd been tested and tested and tested. We knew all too well."

"So why did we keep making them, if we knew?"

"For balance."

"What kind of balance?"

"As it turned out," a pained look comes to his face as he remembers, "the only thing *balanced* was the destruction. At the time, though, they talked about a balance of power—balanced forces. Even the leaders who were most serious about reducing our weapons didn't seem to think *we* could unless Russia did."

"Why? Would they have done this even if we hadn't done it to them?" The girl looks doubtfully at the old man.

"Oh, I don't suppose so; they wouldn't have needed to." Then he adds, "They could have taken us without firing a shot. That's what everyone was afraid of. No one wanted to be a red."

"A red?" The girl looks puzzled for a second. Then her eyes light up. "Oh, like the bumper stickers we used to see: Better dead than red!"

"Yup."

"What's a red? How could that be worse than this?"

"Communist tyranny—someone else deciding for you how you'll live and work and believe. Some people think that's worse than being dead."

"Yes, but what about those people who don't think that? What about my family who didn't *get* to decide. That isn't fair. Somebody else already decided for them. Only they didn't decide for them how they'll live; they decided how they'll die. *That's* tyranny!"

"Well," the old man looks glum, "I don't suppose anybody thought they'd actually *have* to choose between dead and red. And now, whether we're red or not, there probably won't be much freedom for a long, long time. I don't know who won. I doubt if it matters anymore."

"Were they—the reds, I mean—were they trying to take over our government?"

The old man shakes his head with an ironic smile. "No, they were just trying to take over some of the oil fields in the Middle East."

"And those governments asked *us* for protection?"

"No, they didn't ask, but we felt we had the right."

"To their oil?"

"To protect it."

"Why?"

"We thought we needed it for our way of life."

"Our way of life," she says sarcastically, "and now it's gone forever."

They are silent for a while. Everything is silent. The old man suddenly realizes he hasn't heard or seen any birds since the explosion. Several minutes pass. He breaks the silence. "It wasn't that we didn't know the weapons were dangerous. We just thought the ends justified the means."

"What are ends and means?"

"We thought our loaded weapons were the only means to peace. But when we used these weapons, they were the means to the most terrible end possible."

"Why didn't someone try to stop it? The people in the churches should have spoken up."

"Oh, some did," the old man responds, "but mostly their ideas weren't much different from anyone else's. They thought war was okay as long as it was justified. Their ideas changed a lot slower than the weapons did, so a lot of them never realized *this* would never be justified."

"But surely, good Christian people couldn't help to do something this awful without knowing it was wrong!"

"That's what we said about Christians in Hitler's Germany too. I guess as long as someone *else* tells them to do something, people think they're not responsible for what happens." He sighs and adds, "A lot of Christians just didn't think God would let this happen to us."

"Well, they were wrong!"

"Yeah, and then others thought this was bound to happen—that God would punish us, and nothing we could do would stop it."

"But that doesn't make sense! If they were helping to do something wrong, how could they blame God? How could Christian people keep from seeing how wrong it all was?"

"Somehow a lot of them didn't think that being a Christian had anything to do with weapons—it wasn't a spiritual matter. I don't know why. Abortion was—and pornography." He looks at the girl and wonders whether she knows about those things. "But the weapons—they seemed like a 'necessary' evil. Everyone wanted to be realistic."

"They don't seem a *bit* realistic now."

"No, nothing seems the same." He thinks awhile. "The people we used to think were totally unrealistic were saying we should love our enemies and return good for evil and pray for our enemies. I think now that's the only thing that could have kept this from happening. But most Christians just thought it seemed too dangerous."

"If they hadn't been so afraid to try," the girl says sadly, "maybe things could have turned out differently."

# *Notes*

## *Chapter 1*

1. Billy Graham interview, "A Change of Heart: Billy Graham on the Nuclear Arms Race," *Sojourners*, Aug. 1979, p. 14.

2. Robert F. Kennedy, *Thirteen Days: A Memoir of the Cuban Missile Crisis* (New York: W. W. Norton, 1969), p. 106.

3. Billy Graham, op. cit.

## *Chapter 2*

1. Alan Kreider, "The Pacifism of the Early Church," in *A Matter of Faith* (Washington, D.C.: *Sojourners*, 1981), pp. 44-45.

2. *Ante-Nicene Fathers*, Vol. IV (Grand Rapids, Mich.: Eerdmans, 1965), pp. 395-669.

3. J. C. Wenger, *The Way of Peace* (Scottdale, Pa.: Herald Press, 1977), p. 19.

4. *Ibid.*, p. 21.

5. *Ibid.*, p. 22.

## *Chapter 3*

1. Vernard Eller, *War and Peace from Genesis to Revelation* (Scottdale, Pa.: Herald Press, 1981), pp. 70-71.

2. For a fuller discussion, see Guy F. Hershberger, *War, Peace, and Nonresistance* (Scottdale, Pa.: Herald Press, 1953), pp. 28-31.

3. Peter C. Craigie, *The Problem of War in the Old Testament* (Grand Rapids, Mich.: Eerdmans, 1978), pp. 106-07.

## Chapter 4

1. Eller, p. 146.
2. Ronald J. Sider, *Christ and Violence* (Scottdale, Pa.: Herald Press, 1979), pp. 33-35.

## Chapter 5

1. Joseph Fletcher, *Situation Ethics: The New Morality* (Philadelphia: Westminster Press, 1966), pp. 164-65.
2. Francis A. Schaeffer, *How Should We Then Live?* (Old Tappan, N.J.: Revell, 1976), pp. 218-23.
3. *Ibid.*, p. 205.
4. Richard S. Taylor, "A Theology of War and Peace as Related to Perfect Love: A Case for Participation in War," in *Perfect Love and War*, ed. Paul Hostetler (Nappanee, Ind.: Evangel Press, 1974), p. 29.

## Chapter 6

1. Eller, pp. 59-60.
2. Catherine Marshall, *Something More* (New York: McGraw-Hill, 1974), pp. 256-57.

## Chapter 7

1. Paul N. Ellis, "The Christian as Peacemaker," in *Perfect Love and War*, pp. 78-79.

## Chapter 8

1. Father George Zabelka interview, "I Was Told It Was Necessary," *Sojourners* (Aug. 1980), pp. 14-15.
2. Marshall, pp. 225-26.

# *The Author*

Duane Beachey's peacemaking effort goes beyond opposing war to include active involvement in working with the poor and the elderly. Since 1975 he and his wife Gloria and their two daughters—Carissa, age seven, and Sarah, age four—have been involved in the Mennonite Voluntary Service program, working with the housing needs of low-income and elderly people in Oklahoma City. The Mennonite church they attend has joined with six black Baptist churches and a Christian Church to work together to alleviate critical housing needs in their community.

Duane was born and raised in Illinois, attended Hesston College in Kansas and Goshen College in In-

diana, and spent one year at the Associated Mennonite
Biblical Seminary in Elkhart, Indiana.

He has helped bring together a group of people of differing backgrounds from around Oklahoma City who
are interested in various aspects of peacemaking: Meth-
odists, Catholics, Friends, Disciples, Mennonites, and
others. The purpose of this group is to develop ways of
raising the issue of peacemaking in schools, churches,
colleges, and through the media.

He has been involved in leading workshops through
various churches, challenging Christians of all denominations to be peacemakers.

# *The Christian Peace Shelf*

The Christian Peace Shelf is a selection of Herald Press books and pamphlets devoted to the promotion of Christian peace principles and their applications. The editor (appointed by the Mennonite Central Committee Peace Section) and an editorial board from the Brethren in Christ Church, the General Conference Mennonite Church, the Mennonite Brethren Church, and the Mennonite Church, represent the historic concern for peace within these constituencies.

*For Serious Study*

Durland, William R. *No King but Caesar?* (1975). A Catholic lawyer looks at Christian violence.

Enz, Jacob J. *The Christian and Warfare* (1972). The roots of pacifism in the Old Testament.

Hershberger, Guy F. *War, Peace, and Nonresistance* (Third Edition, 1969). A classic comprehensive work on nonresistance in faith and history.

Hornus, Jean-Michel. *It Is Not Lawful for Me to Fight*